THE BODY AND ULTIMATE CONCERN

MERCER UNIVERSITY PRESS

Endowed by

TOM WATSON BROWN
and
THE WATSON-BROWN FOUNDATION, INC.

THE BODY AND ULTIMATE CONCERN

Reflections on an Embodied Theology of Paul Tillich

EDITED BY

ADAM PRYOR AND DEVAN STAHL

Mercer University Press | Macon, Georgia
2018

MUP/ H958

© 2018 by Mercer University Press
Published by Mercer University Press
1501 Mercer University Drive
Macon, Georgia 31207
All rights reserved

9 8 7 6 5 4 3 2 1

Books published by Mercer University Press are printed on acid-free paper
that meets the requirements of the American National Standard for
Information Sciences—Permanence of Paper for Printed Library Materials.

Printed and bound in the United States.

This book is set in Adobe Caslon

ISBN   978-0-88146-682-9
Cataloging-in-Publication Data is available from the Library of Congress

Contents

.

Contributors

MARY ANN STENGER, Professor Emerita in Humanities, University of Louisville, is a co-author of *Dialogues of Paul Tillich* (Mercer University Press) and of more than twenty journal articles and book chapters on Tillich. She serves as a co-editor of the *International Yearbook for Tillich Research* and the *Tillich Research* series (both through W. de Gruyter).

DAVID H. NIKKEL earned his Ph.D. from Duke University and is Professor and Department Chair of Philosophy and Religion at the University of North Carolina, Pembroke. A long-time researcher in the work of both Paul Tillich and Michael Polanyi, his recent research has focused on issues of embodiment and panentheism as most thoroughly explored in his book *Radical Embodiment* (Wipf & Stock, 2010).

KAYKO DRIEDGER HESSLEIN has a Ph.D. in Systematic Theology from the Graduate Theological Union, Berkeley. She is an ordained minister in the Evangelical Lutheran Church in Canada, serving as an interim pastor and also teaching at Lutheran Theological Seminary (Saskatoon) and Waterloo Lutheran Seminary. Her book, *Dual Citizenship* (T&T Clark), was published in 2015.

BETH RITTER-CONN holds a Ph.D. in Systematic and Philosophical Theology from the Graduate Theological Union in Berkeley, California. She is a lecturer in the Honors Program and the College of Theology and Christian Ministry at Belmont University in Nashville, Tennessee.

TYLER ATKINSON holds a Ph.D. from the University of Aberdeen and an M.Div. from Duke Divinity School. He is Assistant Professor of Religion at Bethany College (Lindsborg, KS). His current research lies at the intersection of theological ethics, critical race theory, and hip hop studies.

COURTNEY WILDER earned her Ph.D. from the University of Chicago and is Associate Professor of Religion at Midland University in Freemont, Nebraska. She has published numerous articles on the theology of Paul Tillich and disability theology. Her newest work, *Disability, Faith, and the Church* (Praeger, 2016), combines elements of these research interests.

ADAM PRYOR is Assistant Professor of Religion and Director of Core Education at Bethany College (Lindsborg, KS). His research has focused on the role of the body in construing religious phenomena within Christianity and the constructive use of Paul Tillich's theology as it relates to issues in Religion and Science, as with his books *The God Who Lives* (Pickwick, 2014) and *Body of Christ Incarnate for You* (Lexington, 2016).

DEVAN STAHL is Assistant Professor of Clinical Ethics in the Center for Ethics and Humanities in the Life Sciences at Michigan State University. Dr. Stahl received her Ph.D. in Health Care Ethics from Saint Louis University and her M.Div. from Vanderbilt University. Dr. Stahl's research focuses on the intersections of theology and medicine and her recent book is *Imaging and Interpreting Illness: Becoming Whole in a Broken Body* (Cascade Books, 2018).

Acknowledgments

There are so many people to thank when producing an edited volume such as this. We are very grateful to each of our contributors; their patience, hard work, and commitment to seeing this volume through to completion has made it a joy to work with each of them. In addition, we would like to thank Kaylie Ines who did significant copy-editing and proof reading; Michigan State University who supported us financially through a HARP Production Grant; and to Marc Jolley and Mercer University Press for their commitment to publishing the project. Perhaps most of all though, we are thankful for the encouragement and support we received from the North American Paul Tillich Society, especially Fred Parrella and Mary Ann Stenger. What started as a series of interesting conference papers would not have been anything more than that without the repeated encouragement we received from this group of scholars.

Introduction

MARY ANN STENGER

One of the lasting legacies of Paul Tillich is the incorporation of some of his ideas into ongoing constructive theological work. This collection on the body and ultimate concern exemplifies this, as the authors critique, modify, and employ several of Tillich's theological insights. In one sense, the very universalizing direction of his thought grounds this work, even as several authors reject that direction in favor of more specific contextual theology. Their constructive efforts offer exciting new approaches to the topic of the body as well as to Tillich.

In the several decades since Paul Tillich's death in 1965, the topic of the body has been central in several different contemporary theologies that arise out of particular contexts. The issue of the role and the treatment of the body arises in feminist, womanist, disability, Black, Asian, and other social and religious contexts. In contrast to these specific approaches, Tillich worked with a more universal approach to philosophical and theological thinking while his ideas also helped to foster some of these contextual theologies. Foremost in this influence has been his method of correlation, with its recognition of the importance of the concrete situation, and also his understanding of symbols and the role of experience influencing theology. In this book, the focus is on Tillich's understanding of ultimate concern in relationship to human bodies, but many of the essays incorporate other aspects of Tillich's theology in their effort to develop an embodied theology of Paul Tillich.

Tillich did not discuss the human body at any length, but he assumed it in his understanding of ultimate concern and more broadly in his theology of culture. Although his wife Hannah reported that Tillich had a strong interest in female bodies, that does not manifest in his theology. Rather, the cognitive, philosophical dimension of human being dominates his thought.

Yet, the body appears indirectly in Tillich's work. In the area of ethics, for instance, Tillich offers a very insightful understanding of the role of the body in human interactions with respect to the dimension of power. He argues that in every human encounter, "power is active, the power of the personal radiation, expressed in language and gestures, in the glance of the eye and the sound of the voice, in face and figure and movement, expressed in what one is personally and what one represents socially."[1] He goes on to argue that human struggles about power "start in the life of an individual in the moment of his conception and go on up to the moment of his last breath."[2] Moreover, he states that the specific power that one has is related to one's specific type or power of being, "a plant and not a stone, a beast and not a tree, a man and not a dog, a female and not a male."[3] These arguments suggest that, for Tillich, one cannot separate one's power of being in relation to others or one's social power from one's specific body, even though he does not state that directly.

Tillich is even more indirect about our bodies throughout most of his theology—assuming the fact of the body as part of being human but seldom referring to it. This occurs in part because he thinks about humanity as a whole in relation to culture or to

---

[1] Paul Tillich, *Love, Power, and Justice* (New York: Oxford University Press, 1960) 87.

[2] Ibid.

[3] Ibid., 88.

history, all in broad terms. Clearly, only embodied humans are the enactors of culture and history, but that fact of embodiment mattered little to Tillich's thought. While his own embodiment mattered greatly to his life, whether in the trenches in World War I or in his personal relationships, he offers little self-reflection on the body.

In his various autobiographical presentations, he speaks of his romantic connection to nature but describes his participation in nature as "aesthetic-meditative" or mystical[4] or as opening up philosophical understanding.[5] He speaks of his strong ties to the country, mentioning not only what he saw but also what he smelled.[6] He describes his experiences of the sea as influential on his thinking. For example, he ties his understanding of the boundary situation directly to his "experience of the infinite bordering on the finite" with the sea.[7] He states: "The sea also supplied the imaginative element necessary for the doctrines of the Absolute as both ground and abyss of dynamic truth, and of the substance of religion as the thrust of the eternal into finitude. …Many of my ideas were conceived in the open and much of my writing done among trees or by the sea."[8] In a later reflection, he compares his experience of the sea to the impression big cities (e.g., Berlin and New York) made on him: "infinity, openness, unrestricted space!"[9] His experience of a place seems to focus mostly on his inner reflec-

---

[4] Paul Tillich, "Autobiographical Reflections," *The Theology of Paul Tillich*, ed. Charles W. Kegley and Robert W. Bretall (New York: The Macmillan Company, 1964) 4–5.

[5] Paul Tillich, "What Am I?" *My Search for Absolutes*, ed. Ruth Nanda Anshen (New York: Simon and Schuster, 1969) 29. Also see Paul Tillich, *On the Boundary* (New York: Charles Scribner's Sons, 1966) 18.

[6] Tillich, *On the Boundary*, 17.

[7] Ibid., 18.

[8] Ibid.

[9] Tillich, "What Am I?", 29.

tions on being there rather than his bodily experience of its particular characteristics.

Thus, connecting the body to ultimate concern or faith was not central to Tillich's theology. But as he suggests, his emphasis on ultimacy as part of defining religion and faith stemmed from his experiences of infinity in nature. His inclusion of "concern" in his definition of religion "points to the 'existential' character of religious experience."[10] Experience is central to ultimate concern for Tillich, and what the essays in this volume contribute is analysis of the bodily dimension of that experience.

Paul Tillich's idea of religion or faith as ultimate concern is probably known to most undergraduates who have taken an Introduction to Religion course and certainly to most scholars of Religious Studies. Religion theorist Jonathan Z. Smith has argued that Tillich's idea of ultimate concern provided a language for the development of religious studies in North American colleges and universities.[11] Even the Supreme Court of the United States used Tillich's idea of ultimate concern in its 1965 decision affirming Mr. Seeger's request for conscientious objector status even though he did not connect with a religious institution.[12]

When Tillich defines faith as "the state of being ultimately concerned," in *Dynamics of Faith*, he also states that it involves the "total personality" and "happens in the center of the personal life and includes all its elements."[13] But Tillich does not explicitly discuss a person's body as part of one's personal life. Certainly, he assumes the body as a part of a person's being; yet, much of his

---

[10] Paul Tillich, *Systematic Theology*, 3 vols. (Chicago: The University of Chicago Press, 1951–1963) 1:12.

[11] Jonathan Z. Smith, "Tillich['s] Remains...," *Journal of the American Academy of Religion* 78/4 (December 2010): 1139.

[12] *United States v. Seeger*, 380, U.S. 187, 1965.

[13] Paul Tillich, *Dynamics of Faith* (New York: Harper & Row, 1957) 4.

discussion of ultimate concern ignores the body and its role in faith and religious life. Thus, Adam Pryor and Devan Stahl with their contributors have opened up important bodily dimensions of ultimate concern, both affirming and critiquing aspects of Tillich's approach.

As their essays attest, the academy has given increased attention to embodiment over the last several decades, in ways that Tillich could not have imagined. Focus on our bodies includes attention to race, ethnicity, bio-medical issues, disability, sexuality, and more. By bringing Tillich into dialogue with several theories and theologies of embodiment, they both highlight the assumptions about bodies implicit in Tillich and show to what extent his theology can be helpful to current discussions as well as points that need to be modified or even rejected.

Both "ultimate" and "concern" matter to Tillich's definition of faith as "the state of being ultimately concerned." As he explains it, if something claims ultimacy in one's life, it "demands the total surrender" and "promises total fulfillment."[14] All other demands and concerns are subordinate to what one experiences as ultimate. The element of concern points to the inclusion of intellect, will, and emotion in the experience of faith, but any role for the body is ignored. Ultimate concern involves the whole personality, including both conscious and unconscious elements, rational and non-rational aspects, and yet transcends those elements as an ecstatic act and experience.[15] This emphasis on the whole personality shows the subjective side of ultimate concern, but the element of ultimacy points to the objective meaning in faith. As Tillich points out, "almost every thing 'in heaven and on earth' has received ulti-

---

[14] Ibid., 1.
[15] Ibid., 5–6.

macy in the history of human religion."[16] So the challenge is judging what is truly ultimate over against ordinary finite things that may claim to be ultimate.

Although Tillich describes ultimate concern as an act, it certainly is more than just one act. As he states in *The Courage to Be*: "Faith is not an opinion but a state. It is the state of being grasped by the power of being which transcends everything that is and in which everything that is participates."[17] Ultimate concern is a state of being that affects all one's actions, decisions, and responses to the world. To be in that state of ultimate concern assumes that one has a body, but Tillich makes little reference to that. He does speak of biological aspects of anxiety, courage, and spirituality: "Every cell of his body participates in his freedom and spirituality, and every act of his spiritual creativity is nourished by his vital dynamics."[18] Yet that affirmation of the importance of the body to spiritual life does not lead to further discussion of the body in anxiety, courage, and faith. Once again, a person's body is assumed but not reflected on in Tillich's theology. In none of this does Tillich consider what impact people's diverse bodies might have on their spiritual lives.

In fact, when Tillich speaks about spiritual life, he argues that "[L]ife as spirit transcends the duality of body and mind" as well as "the triplicity of body, soul, and mind."[19] For him, the human spirit is directly connected to the divine Spirit or what he calls in the third volume of his *Systematic Theology*, Spiritual Presence. A person's spirit involves self-transcendence in the experience of being

---

[16] Tillich, *Dynamics of Faith*, 10.

[17] Paul Tillich, *The Courage to Be* (New Haven: Yale University Press, 1952) 173.

[18] Ibid., 83.

[19] Tillich, *Systematic Theology*, 1:250.

"grasped by something ultimate and unconditional."[20] One's body is necessary to that experience, but Tillich ignores any bodily aspects of that experience. Yet, if life includes body and mind, and ultimate concern involves more than the mind or intellect, then body would be important to faith, for Tillich, although he sees the duality as transcended.

But even if Tillich merely assumes the fact of one's body in faith/ultimate concern, what about his understanding of Jesus as incarnate? Tillich expresses problems with the term "Incarnation," rejecting what he sees as "pagan" or "superstitious" meanings attached to it. He does accept the Johannine affirmation that the "Logos became flesh," but even here he shies away from what we usually think of as our flesh, our bodies. "'Flesh' does not mean a material substance but stands for historical existence."[21] His preferred understanding of "Incarnation" is that "God is manifest in a personal life process as a saving participant in the human predicament."[22] With that understanding, Tillich then allows for other incarnations or "possible divine manifestations in other areas or periods of being."[23] When he shifts from doctrine to the event of Jesus as the Christ, he clearly accepts that Jesus was born and died.[24] But his focus is not on Jesus as a human person with a body but on his activity and reception as the Christ, the New Being. Moreover, Tillich argues that "Jesus could not have been the Christ without sacrificing himself as Jesus to himself as the Christ."[25] The crucifixion dominates Tillich's understanding of Jesus as the Christ; in the crucifixion, Jesus' body (and also the

---

[20] Ibid., 3:112.
[21] Ibid., 2:95.
[22] Ibid.
[23] Ibid., 2:96.
[24] Ibid., 2:148.
[25] Tillich, *Dynamics of Faith*, 97–98.

particulars of his historical existence) are sacrificed in order to reveal Jesus as the Christ.

Given all the above considerations, Tillich's theology might not seem a likely source for discussing embodied life theologically. At best, he assumes the body in human life, and at worst, he ignores it in favor of mind and spirit. With Jesus, he prefers a symbolic understanding of Jesus as the Christ or New Being in spite of his emphasis on Jesus in history. But the importance of this collection is that the authors discuss much more than Tillich's few statements about the body. Instead, they pull from many aspects of Tillich's theology (method of correlation, Christology, ontology, symbols, faith, and courage) and bring his ideas into dialogue with contemporary discussions of the body.

Tillich grounds his theology in his ultimate concern with the Christian message and notes that such ultimate concern does not preclude critique and even rejection of aspects of that message.[26] But even with critique, it will be the ultimate concern that leads to the critique. In a sense, ultimate concern surpasses the content of the Christian message because the content itself can be subject to doubt. What is of ultimate concern determines one's being or not-being in relation to the whole of reality and to the meaning of existence itself.[27] Ultimate concern grounds and yet is deeper than the ordinary, preliminary concerns of life.

Because ultimate concern is central to Tillich's theology, it connects to all areas of his thought—epistemology, theology of culture, Christology, ethics, and more. Especially in his widely accessible *Dynamics of Faith*, Tillich analyzes types of ultimate concern or faith, the relationship of faith to several parts of culture, the contrast of the truth of faith to other kinds of truth, and

---

[26] Tillich, *Systematic Theology*, 1:10.
[27] Ibid., 1:14.

the connection of individual ultimate concern to a community of faith. In making these connections, Tillich sets up the possibility of conversations between science and religion, psychology and faith, and faith and ethics such as the authors engage in here. Their discussions do not privilege science or other fields over faith but show how the insights of several academic fields enhance our understanding of ourselves and consequently faith.

Tillich supported such engagement, as his approach to science attests. But he never sees the truth of another field impinging on the truth of faith. Tillich notes: "There is no conflict between faith in its true nature and reason in its true nature."[28] He makes this claim because he understands reason as "the basis of language, of freedom, of creativity. ...[I]t makes a centered personal life and a participation in community possible."[29] For Tillich, reason is a necessary condition for having faith, for being "able to be ultimately concerned."[30] Both scientific truth and the truth of faith depend on reason, but, for Tillich, they belong to different dimensions of meaning and should not interfere with each other.[31] Tillich warns against using scientific knowledge to confirm faith as true,[32] but he certainly was open to engaging in discussions with scientists, psychologists, and health professionals as we see in numerous writings.[33] And his comments about keeping the truth of faith in its own dimension and scientific truth in its sphere can

---

[28] Tillich, *Dynamics of Faith*, 80.
[29] Ibid., 75.
[30] Ibid., 76.
[31] Ibid., 81.
[32] Ibid., 85.
[33] For example, see Tillich, *The Courage to Be*, 64–85; Paul Tillich, *Theology of Culture* (London, Oxford, New York: Oxford University Press, 1959) 112–32; Tillich, *Dynamics of Faith*, 4–5, 80–89; Paul Tillich, *The Meaning of Health: Essays in Existentialism, Psychoanalysis, and Religion*, ed. Perry Le Fevre (Chicago: Exploration Press, 1984).

apply to truth in other spheres of culture as well. None of the articles here privilege the truth from the specific spheres of culture they engage as higher than the truth of faith. Rather, they critically engage ideas from these varying cultural areas in dialogue with critical engagement of Tillich's ideas.

By way of introducing the specific articles of this volume, I shall focus on what aspects of Tillich's thought the authors engage to develop an embodied theology. Throughout they show appreciation for Tillich's insights but also offer critique of his ideas, as I believe he would have wanted and thought necessary. In a certain sense, all of the authors here employ Tillich's method of correlation where the theologian attempts to correlate the questions implied in the present situation of human existence with answers given in the Christian message.[34] Tillich begins his later *Systematic Theology* with the argument that the theologian has the task of interpreting the truth of the Christian message for his or her own generation.[35] Thus, Tillich would have expected theologians of the early twenty-first century to address the questions of their own time. This clearly is the task that this volume's authors have taken very seriously, with each author focusing on a different aspect of the body or specific question that an embodied theology must address.

Since the authors cover such diverse aspects of human bodies, they show the complexity of our bodies and of the issues connecting to them. They cover the interconnection of bodies and language, the role of bodies in knowledge and faith, the multiplicity of bodies and their multiple relationships including participation in rituals of diverse religious traditions, the issues of hunger and food insecurity, Black male bodies in American culture, disabled

---

[34] Tillich, *Systematic Theology*, 1:8.
[35] Ibid., 1:3.

bodies in relation to sin and faith, technologically enhanced bodies, and issues of post-humanism and transhumanism. Unlike Tillich who mostly assumes the fact of embodiment, these authors place embodiment at the center of religious life and theology. Together, they offer an embodied theology with insights from Tillich's theology.

David Nikkel brings Tillich's idea of ultimate concern into dialogue with biological, neuro-scientific, and linguistic approaches to the mind to develop his own normative theory about the nature of religion. He argues that the body mediates our knowledge, language, and actions, grounding an intuitive ultimate concern in people's everyday embodied living. He incorporates Tillich's idea that humans become aware of the divine or ultimacy "only through experience of particular finite realities" (34). But for Tillich the finite reality is simply the trigger for the awareness of the infinite, with both the particulars of the finite reality and the embodied dimension of the experience becoming irrelevant. In contrast, Nikkel affirms the importance of the bodily dimension and the sacred goodness of embodied life.

In her critique of Tillich's ontology, Kayko Driedger Hesslein focuses on his discussion of the polarities of individualization and participation, dynamics and form, and freedom and destiny. For her, all three polarities show "a tension between particularity and universality," but Tillich is too concerned about "overdetermination by particularity" (43) and fails to appreciate multiplicity in relation to bodies. She argues for recognizing multiplicity not only among bodies but within one body and addresses this in relation to "multiply-religious bodies" who participate in rituals of diverse religious communities. She does see a possible resolution for this problem in Tillich's theology through his understanding of concreteness and universality in relation to Jesus as the Christ or New

Being.

Beth Ritter-Conn focuses on Tillich's discussion of non-being and anxiety in relation to hunger and food insecurity. She agrees with Tillich that everyone experiences the threat of non-being but argues that "non-being threatens beings differently" (66), with particular focus on those who face food insecurity on a daily basis. She brings Tillich's ideas of anxiety, estrangement, and contingency into dialogue with Judith Butler's ideas of vulnerability, precariousness, and precarity. Because food often takes on religious or social meanings beyond its material value, Ritter-Conn argues that it easily becomes a source of anxiety and symptom of estrangement. With Tillich's idea of persons within a community of persons, she discusses local and global interdependence and calls for a deepening sense of love and solidarity.

Tyler Atkinson uses Tillich's ideas of ultimate concern, the religious symbol of the Cross, and the courage to be as oneself to explore the Black body through the music and imagery of hip-hop artist Tupac Shakur. Atkinson analyzes Tupac's thug spirituality as a focus on embodied life as a Black male in the ghetto. He explores Tillich's analysis of the symbolism of the Cross and the anxiety of meaninglessness in Pablo Picasso's art as useful in understanding Tupac's imagery of the cross. Atkinson then connects Tupac's image of black men on the cross of the Christ with the theology of James Cone; both express the challenging situation of people of color in the United States. Atkinson points out the despair and self-hatred expressed by Tupac and yet his perseverance and courage to be as oneself.

Courtney Wilder explores the tensions in Tillich's understanding of Christ as the New Being and Christ as Healer in relationship to the issue of disability. She shows that in both his sermons and his *Systematic Theology*, Tillich identifies sin with the need for psychological and physical healing. She argues that his association of wholeness and health with salvation implies a negative view of people's disabilities, even connecting them with sin. By incorporating ideas from the theologies of Nancy Eiesland, Thomas Reynolds, and John Swinton, Wilder shows the problems in Tillich's approach to disability and the need for correcting it. Still, she finds value in Tillich's method of correlation, his life story, and his critique of idolatry and uses these to reinterpret the symbol of Christ as Healer.

Adam Pryor engages ethical issues of technology to analyze the implications of cyborgs or technologically enhanced bodies in relation to post-humanism and Tillich's idea of ultimate concern. Because cyborg bodies offer particular unifications of self and world, Pryor suggests that potentially the cyborg body could reveal ultimate concern. He argues that Tillich's four principles of justice (adequacy, equality, personality, and liberty) must be met in efforts to unify self and world and in any true ultimate concern. He does recognize the ambiguities in cyborg bodies, but he also suggests that cyborg bodies can be linked to Tillich's vision of essentialization that moves beyond the distortions of ordinary finite life and to his understanding of final revelation.

Devan Stahl analyzes the Christian transhumanist movement through Tillich's approach to technology, ultimate concern, and idolatry. She notes that it is not surprising that many Christian transhumanists quote Tillich in support of their arguments, as Tillich did not see science and religion as opposed to each other but rather working in different spheres of meaning. But Stahl recognizes that Tillich's appreciation for science did not mean a noncritical approach, and she appreciates his recognition that sometimes proponents of science make faith claims that can create conflict. By applying Tillich's emphasis on ambiguity in all human endeavors along with his critique of idolatry, Stahl offers a nuanced approach to Christian transhumanism and calls for caution in full acceptance of it.

From concerns about bodily integrity to considering bodies on the margins of society to discussions of technologically modified bodies, these articles offer us fresh theological insights and call us to ethical thinking and actions in relation to our bodies and the bodies around us. And certainly, today, the body and a person's right to bodily integrity have become central, critical issues in our culture. We must think theologically and ethically about bodies in an effort to probe more deeply into the issues than the more sensationalized approaches in the news.

I am grateful to these authors for their theological work, and I am honored to have been asked to contribute to this volume with my introduction. Work on Tillich's thought has engaged me since my undergraduate days, and yet I continue to be amazed and gratified at the ways in which his thought stimulates younger scholars of religion. I doubt that Tillich could have imagined "an embodied theology of Paul Tillich," but the articles in this volume do justice to his thought and to his commitment that theology must address the questions arising out of the existential and cultural situation of its own time.

I

Embodying Ultimate Concern

DAVID H. NIKKEL

Human beings are radically embodied. Our bodies root us in the world. They orient our every experience of the world—enabling us to engage the various natural and social elements of the world, often without our conscious or explicit realization. Moreover, in so doing our bodies enable us to experience the ever-present affective and aesthetic dimensions of our engagement with the world; it is through the distinctive qualities of our bodies that the world appears to us as intelligible or knowable and valuable.

As a biological organism, the body is differentiated from but consonant with its environment, as it makes real contact with that environment, with other bodies and physical realities. Indeed, as sentient organism, the body constitutes the very correlation of subjectivity and objectivity. The body is a self-organizing system, always in correlation with the dynamic systems of its environment. Body and environment co-define or co-specify each other in some fashion. The embodied self never exists in a "pure" state, which is in complete isolation from any environment. And as long as the self-organizing body endures, it always has some effect, even if a small one, on its environment. Evolutionarily speaking, organisms, including sentient ones, have evolved to have some basic "fit" with their environment, to attune to that environment so as to survive and even thrive. This suggests that animals experience a basic at-

home-ness or sense of belonging in the world. The normal experience of animals, then, including humans from infancy, is one of
living in a meaningful world, rather than that of being thrown into
existence and tasked with completely manufacturing meaning, as
some existentialists and constructivists would have it.

This chapter will first develop the claim alluded to above that
human beings are radically embodied. The body serves as the root
of sentience and of all meaning as it is always in correlation with
an environment. In turn, language relies upon embodied schemas,
and the body as correlation of subjectivity and objectivity mediates
all our knowing and acting with an "inner teleology." Next, the
chapter will reconstitute Tillich's concept of ultimate concern in
terms of such an understanding of human embodiment. To do so,
I will draw extensively upon neuroscientist Antonio Damasio's
notion of background feelings in relation to a sense of bodily integrity and upon the nature of human and animal attempts to orient ourselves to our environment, referencing ecological psychology, emergence theory, and phenomenologies of the body.
Orienting the insights from these diverse fields around Tillich's
understanding of ultimate concern, I conclude that humans and
other animals *manifest an intuitive ultimate concern in their normal
bodily integrity and orientation to an environment.* That concern can
become reflective in human beings, perhaps providing a basis for a
contemporary normative theory about the nature of religion.

HUMANS AS RADICALLY EMBODIED

Ecological psychologist James J. Gibson described the meaningful embodiment of sentient organisms, particularly things that
possess sensorimotor meaning, in terms of "affordances" the environment supplies, involving a joint project of organism and envi-

ronment.[1] Crucially, Gibson's development of the idea of affordances entails that perception is not a neutral cognition just of objects and spatiality, but cognition of value in the environment both for good and for ill for an organism. Philosopher of cognitive science and mind, Evan Thompson, writes of sentient cognition as inherently involving the values of a self-organizing body acting in its milieu: "Cognition is behavior or conduct in relation to meaning and norms that the system itself enacts or brings forth on the basis of its autonomy."[2] Or in a similar vein, "a cognitive being's world is not a prespecified, external realm, represented internally by its brain, but a relational domain enacted or brought forth by that being's autonomous agency and mode of coupling with the environment."[3] Biologist Terrence Deacon adumbrates that life processes of an organism interacting with its environment entail "teleodynamics," in which *telos* or ends, goals, purpose, or function emerge, and that in conscious organisms awareness of *telos* emerges.[4] Philosopher Mark Johnson puts it this way: "An embodied view of meaning looks for the origins and structures of meaning in the organic activities of embodied creatures in interaction with their changing environments."[5] From different disciplines, all these thinkers reject any notion that meaning arises from an internalized conscious subject, an objectified external environment, or an interaction that somehow occurs between such disparate entities.

---

[1] James J. Gibson, *The Ecological Approach to Visual Perception* (New York: Houghton Mifflin, 1979).

[2] Evan Thompson, *Mind in Life: Biology, Phenomenology, and the Sciences of Mind* (Cambridge MA: Harvard University Press, 2007) 126.

[3] Ibid., 13.

[4] Terrence W. Deacon, *Incomplete Nature: How Mind Emerged from Matter* (New York: W. W. Norton & Co., 2012).

[5] Mark Johnson, *The Meaning of the Body: The Aesthetics of Human Understanding* (Chicago: University of Chicago Press, 2007) 11.

Instead, they affirm an always meaning-laden correlation of an engaged conscious body (or embodied mind) with its natural and social environment.

Our radical embodiment, then, entails that all meanings are bodily: that no possible human meaning can be completely disembodied. Our bodies, as they orient us and enable us in an environment, constitute the very roots that make possible all our living, knowing, and valuing. Our lived bodies, or "phenomenal" bodies to invoke phenomenologist Maurice Merleau-Ponty's term,[6] or "mindbodies" in the coinage of philosopher of religion and culture William Poteat,[7] serve as the ground for human life. Our bodies ground the ongoing correlation of our attentive, embodied effort to make sense of things and other beings, to make sense of the world, which call us into a mutually constitutive relationship. As such, they limit and define us, while also granting us all our potentialities. Constructivist-essentialist debates are parasitic upon (and typically tacitly assume) the range of possibilities our bodies provide. These potentialities mean that the body always partially constructs its world. At the same time, this construction functions in correlation with a given-ness, not just from the side of the world, but from the body: The given-ness of an individual body—some common to the species, some unique to that individual—sets parameters for how we engage our environment. Clearly, such givenness changes throughout one's life in accordance with one's body, environment, and experiences.

The dependence of all meaning upon the body is never merely instrumental but always substantive. The radicalness of our em-

---

[6] Maurice Merleau-Ponty, *Phenomenology of Perception*, trans. Colin Smith (London: Routledge and Kegan Paul, 1962) 105.

[7] William H. Poteat, *Polanyian Meditations: In Search of a Post-Critical Logic* (Durham NC: Duke University Press, 1985).

bodiment entails that the practical distinction between substantive and instrumental is never absolute, for the nature and aesthetics of the body color all our meanings. Our radical embodiment does not deny the tremendous creativity and the diversity of human culture; it simply recognizes that all culture relies substantively upon bodily meanings. Radical embodiment does not minimize our human capability to forgo pressing bodily needs; it only affirms that such sacrifice draws substantively on other bodily meanings. The body serves as the inescapable and irreplaceable mediator in all our doing and knowing and all our concerns.

This mediating status, however, does not mean that the values we realize lie beyond the mediation (simply extrinsic to it) or that the body is mere means but not end. As the correlation of subjectivity and objectivity, embodied values are not those of a pure subject(ive body) in itself nor of objects in themselves but always of a lived body engaging its world: moving, dancing, seeing colors, viewing spatial relationships and configurations, hearing sounds, pitch, and rhythm, smelling, tasting, touching, feeling warmth and diverse skin sensations, feeling emotions, encountering other embodied selves, sexual desiring and pleasuring, as well as less immediate ideas and images. These experiences of ideas and images by a lived body engaging its world are not directly perceptions of our primary senses, but they rely upon bodily orientation, movement, or emotions in order to mean anything.[8]

---

[8] This entails what Mark C. Taylor terms "intrinsic finality" or "inner teleology." See "Refiguring Religion," *Journal of the American Academy of Religion* 77/1 (March 2009): 114–17. Taylor credits Kant with broaching the concept, noting Kant's example of the living organism and quoting Kant's description of "an organized natural product...in which every part is reciprocally both means and ends. See Immanuel Kant, *Critique of Judgment*, trans. James Meredith (New York: Oxford University Press, 1973) 22; quoted in Taylor, "Refiguring Religion," 115. Similarly, Evan Thompson credits Kant

Much of this reliance upon our bodies is acritical and tacit. That is, we are normally aware of our ubiquitous rootedness in and reliance upon our bodies in only a tacit manner; since we do not usually focus our attention on our bodies, we are not explicitly aware of them. For example, with "simple" seeing, the very complex activity of positioning one's head and focusing one's eye muscles happens below our conscious awareness. In day-to-day living this is necessary and usually benign, indeed, healthy. Neurobiologist Antonio Damasio regards this "hiding of the body" as an "adaptive distraction," meaning that we are "distracted" from directly attending to our bodies so we can attend to our environment.[9] When this tacit dimension is assumed but not acknowledged in culture, philosophy, and religion, however, we become vulnerable to dualistic and discarnate pictures of human knowing and human nature.

Among our senses, vision especially can allow us to imagine ourselves as discarnate: as though we can see everything in an instant with complete clarity. Many Renaissance paintings provide a good example. Often these paintings make everything in the foreground and background equally clear. The effect is to encourage the viewer to abscond from his or her embodied engagement, as we "lose sight" (pun intended) of how our actual vision involves our muscles and eyes moving to focus on different parts of a scene as time elapses. This crystal-clear perspective hides our bodily eyes and we adopt a God's-eye view of things from a distance.[10]

---

with recognizing the "intrinsically teleological" nature of an organism as "a self-organizing being...that is both cause and effect of itself." See *Mind in Life*, 129–30.

[9] Antonio R. Damasio, *The Feeling of What Happens* (New York: Harcourt Brace & Co., 1999) 29.

[10] Maurice Merleau-Ponty, *The Prose of the World*, trans. John O'Neill (Evanston IL: Northwestern University Press, 1973) 149–50; Poteat, *Polany-*

We find the discarnate perspective of Renaissance painting also echoed in a strand of epistemology. Descartes' positing of a disembodied mind finding certainty in its own subjectivity in contradistinction to extended material objects initiates this trend. However, such a picture continues to inform contemporary viewpoints, as with some forms of social constructivism, which all too often ignore the constraints on human bodies. Additionally, the hope of some to achieve immortality by having the contents of our consciousness uploaded on a super computer; the absolutizing of some subjects in contrast to purportedly grossly physical bodies based on race or gender; the acceptance of relativism and even nihilism in the absence of certain knowledge; and the objectification of humans as meaningless matter and energy in a reductive physicalism—all these represent ways of discarnating us from our lived or phenomenal bodies.

According to philosopher of science and epistemology Michael Polanyi, whose work focused on the "tacit dimension,"[11] our attending or attention in general bears a from-to structure. We attend from tacit and subsidiary particulars proximally—partial meanings or clues—to a focal and holistic meaning of a comprehensive entity distally. What is critical for my purpose here is that the from-to nature of knowing means that knowledge of the totality of what might become explicit—the sum of the parts or proximal particulars—is *not* the same as the comprehensive meaning of a complex whole. The articulated focal meaning of any given part is not the same as that part's tacit meaning in the context of the more comprehensive whole. Polanyi invokes the example of using a hammer as a tool: we focus on the hammer hitting the

---

ian Meditations, 59.

[11] Michael Polanyi, *The Tacit Dimension* (Garden City NY: Doubleday, 1966).

nail, not on the feeling of the hammer on our fingers and palm—
we do not feel that its handle has struck our palm. Yet we are
aware of the feeling of the hammer on our fingers and palm as indirect, subsidiary, instrumental.[12]

Indeed, if we fail to realize this *Gestalt*-like (holistically structured) nature of knowing, we are guaranteed to miss the wider
meaning of things, according to a Polanyian perspective. Striking-
ly, Polanyi notes the problems attendant upon focusing on particulars in performance or action. One example is how a pianist can
lose the music "by concentrating attention on his fingers" or how,
if one repeats a word while focusing on the sound, it becomes
strange, losing its meaning.[13]

The holistic nature of meaning for a living organism indicated here parallels the holistic nature of the organism itself, which,
though involving differentiation within itself, functions as a unit,
wherein the whole is neither identical to nor reducible to the sum
of the parts when their properties are considered linearly, separate-
ly, individually. As the base and basis of all our activity, our body
figures prominently in all tacit knowing: "Our body is the only
assembly of things known almost exclusively by relying on our
awareness of them to attend to something else.... Every time we
make sense of the world, we rely upon tacit knowledge of impacts
made by the world on our body and the complex responses of our
body to these impacts."[14] Indeed, many of the tacit particulars not
so obviously "bodily" as those involved in perception, motion, and

---

[12] Michael Polanyi, *Personal Knowledge: Towards a Post-Critical Philosophy* (Chicago: University of Chicago Press, 1958) 55. As Polanyi puts it,
"subsidiary awareness and focal awareness are mutually exclusive." See *Personal Knowledge*, 56.

[13] Polanyi, *Tacit Dimension*, 18.

[14] Michael Polanyi, *Knowing and Being: Essays by Michael Polanyi*, ed.
Marjorie Grene (Chicago: University of Chicago Press, 1969) 147–48.

feeling not only rely substantively upon these "bodily" particulars, but in some sense also become part of our body. "[W]hen we make a thing function as the proximal term of tacit knowing, we incorporate it in our body—or extend our body to include it—so that we come to dwell in it."[15] This applies to an "external" physical object such as a cane used by a visually impaired person or something more "internal" and mental, as in this quote from phenomenologist Merleau-Ponty:

> I do not need to visualize the word in order to know and pronounce it. It is enough that I possess its articulatory and acoustic style as one of the modulations, one of the possible uses of my body. I reach back for the word as my hand reaches toward the part of my body which is being pricked; the word has a certain location in my linguistic world, and is part of my equipment.[16]

(Both Polanyi and Merleau-Ponty recognize that inside and outside one's body depends upon the context of our knowing, as when looking at one's arm, to use another example.)

THE EMBODIED NATURE OF LANGUAGE AND CULTURE

Human culture, dependent upon symbolic forms, especially language, allows for a plethora of meanings unavailable to other animals (as well as to pre-linguistic infants). Analytic philosophy has tended to admit that only linguistic propositions have meaning, while most other scholarly thinking, even if admitting nonlinguistic bodily meaning, has separated bodily from linguistic meaning and typically subordinated bodily to linguistic meaning. The cultural-linguistic may so pervasively affect our lives that no "pure"

---

[15] Polanyi, *Tacit Dimension*, 16.
[16] Merleau-Ponty, *Phenomenology of Perception*, 180.

bodily experience of the natural world "untainted" by culture exists for language users. Overlooked, however, is the profound, prior, foundational, inalienable effect of the body and nature upon language and culture, especially in the realm of pre-reflective givenness. Indeed, human rationality and language build upon the base of—radically and tacitly rely upon—our bodily being in the world: upon our seeing, hearing, smelling, tactile, motile, emotive, social, sexual bodies. In other words, all language, both semantically and syntactically, relies upon spatial, postural, kinesthetic, perceptual, and emotional body schemas and their metaphorical and metonymic extensions in order to make sense or mean anything. Without bodily schemas language would be nonsensical. We are not then thrown into the world or linguistically constructing the world. As Poteat puts it, "language is structured *upon* and therefore structured *like* our sentiently oriented and motile mind-bodies."[17] All language, then, is body-shaped: evidencing the attunement of self and world through various body schemas.

Mark Johnson (with linguist George Lakoff) argues persuasively for the necessity of non-propositional embodied schemas for the very intelligibility of language. These schemas arise from our perceptual interactions with the world, bodily posture and movements, and manipulation of objects.[18] Many types of schemas orient us spatially. These include the container schema (in-out), the source-path-goal schema (from-to),[19] and bodily projection schemas such as front-back, near-far, left-right, up-down, straight-

---

[17] Poteat, *Polanyian Meditations*, 187–88.

[18] Mark Johnson, *The Body in the Mind: The Bodily Basis of Meaning, Imagination, and Reason* (Chicago: University of Chicago Press, 1987) 29.

[19] Ibid., 30ff; Mark Johnson and George Lakoff, *Philosophy in the Flesh: The Embodied Mind and Its Challenge to Western Thought* (New York: Basic Books, 1999) 31–33.

curved.[20] Force-dynamic schemas rely upon bodily movements and interactions: "pushing, pulling, propelling, supporting, and balance"[21]; compulsion, blockage, counterforce, diversion, removal of restraint, enablement, and attraction.[22] Other less easily categorized schemas are also rooted in bodily interactions with the world, including part-whole, full-empty, mass-count, cycle, iteration, link, contact, and adjacency.[23] Johnson's earlier work tended to leave the impression that each word could be mapped back to a single bodily schema source domain, such as in-out, from-to, enablement, or part-whole.[24] More recently, however, Johnson notes that much of our basic language often stems from combining at least two image schema source domains.[25] Moreover, language not only builds upon basic structural image schemas but also upon "felt qualities" and "vitality affects" of perception, motion, the flow of time, and emotion.[26] Most language we commonly refer to as "literal" metaphorically builds upon one or two bodily image schemas or felt qualities in a fairly straightforward manner. What we commonly recognize as a "metaphor," however, blends several source domains and/or extends the use of the underlying bodily metaphor in novel fashion.[27]

Linguistic syntax permits far-flung extension and manipulation of body schema concepts or perceptual images. Given the abstract nature of syntax, is it plausible that it, too, like semantics

---

[20] Johnson, *Body in the Mind,* 30ff; Johnson and Lakoff, *Philosophy in the Flesh*, 34–35.

[21] Johnson and Lakoff, *Philosophy in the Flesh,* 36.

[22] Johnson, *Body in the Mind,* 44ff.

[23] Ibid., 121–26; Johnson and Lakoff, *Philosophy in the Flesh*, 35.

[24] Edward Slingerland, *What Science Offers the Humanities* (New York: Cambridge University Press, 2008) 174–88.

[25] Johnson, *Meaning of the Body*, 142.

[26] Ibid., 19–28, 41–49, and 143–45.

[27] Ibid., 185.

substantively relies upon our embodiment? Does syntax itself emerge from bodily semantics? And what of mathematics and abstract or formal logic? Nobel Prize-winning neuroscientist Gerald Edelman regards the human ability to place concepts in an ordered relation as an embodied operation present not only in syntax but in a "pre-syntax" of some animals and pre-linguistic infants.[28] Lakoff has categorized examples of this dependency: hierarchical structure stems from part-whole schemas, grammatical and co-reference relations from link schemas, and categories from container (in-out) schemas.[29] Harry Hunt cites psychological experiments supporting the theory that gesture is a key stage of the organization of sentences, externalizing their otherwise implicit spatial design.[30] With regard to mathematics, imagine a disembodied consciousness as a blank slate with no experience of objects: it would have no basis to understand numbers or their ordering. Lakoff, with others, has devoted a book to how mathematics stems from embodied experience of quantity and quantitative relationships.[31] With regard to logic, Johnson notes that William James (and fellow American pragmatist John Dewey, who built upon James's work) "saw that logic lives and moves in embodied experience, and that it cannot be understood apart from purposive human inquiry.... Real logic is embodied—spatial, corporeal, incarnate."[32]

---

[28] Gerald Edelman, *The Remembered Present: A Biological Theory of Consciousness* (New York: Basic Books, 1989) 147.

[29] George Lakoff, *Women, Fire, and Dangerous Things: What Categories Reveal about the Mind* (Chicago: University of Chicago Press, 1987) 289ff.

[30] Harry T. Hunt, *On the Nature of Consciousness: Cognitive, Phenomenological, and Transpersonal Perspectives* (New Haven CT: Yale University Press, 1995) 154–56.

[31] George Lakoff and Raphael E. Nunez, *Where Mathematics Comes From: How the Embodied Mind Brings Mathematics into Being* (New York: Basic Books, 2000).

[32] Johnson, *Meaning of the Body*, 102.

Neuroscientist Damasio holds that *all* knowledge comes embodied in "dispositional representations." Neither Damasio nor Edelman understand mental "representations" as mirrors of a world independent of our enactment.[33] "Dispositional" means that neural networks are patterned in such a way that representations can become active "images," whether visual, auditory, kinesthetic, body-state, or other. Damasio concludes that thought is made up largely of such images. While acknowledging the obvious, that thought includes words and non-image, abstract, arbitrary symbols, he urges that focusing on this truth causes many to miss a converse fact: "both words and arbitrary symbols are based on topographically organized representations and can become images." Indeed, Damasio continues, if our words "did not become images, however fleetingly, they would not be anything we could know."[34] The import of Damasio's words here can hardly be exaggerated: any and all human signs and symbols must involve some connection with bodily sensorimotor and feeling imagery to be comprehensible, indeed to exist in the first place.

ULTIMATE CONCERN AND EMBODIMENT:
BACKGROUND INFORMATION

Tillich's claim that all humans have an ultimate concern and that all human creations manifest an ultimate concern stands as Tillich's most well-known idea. Certainly, it is the one that students in Introduction to Religion classes have encountered the most. The textbook I currently use, Gary Kessler's *Religion: An*

---

[33] For example, see Damasio, *Feeling of What Happens*, 322; Gerald Edelman, *Wider than the Sky: The Phenomenal Gift of Consciousness* (New Haven CT: Yale University Press, 2004) 104ff.

[34] Antonio R. Damasio, *Descartes' Error: Emotion, Reason, and the Human Brain* (New York: G. P. Putnam's Sons) 106.

Introduction through Case Studies, contrasts Tillich's definition or theory of the nature of religion with Melford Spiro's, which centers on superhuman beings.[35] Of course, a Tillichian would note that Spiro's theory tends to reduce the divine to a being, perhaps even the highest being, as opposed to being-itself. I do emphasize that Tillich's theory should not be conflated with the simplistic and way-too-broad theory—a theory that some novice scholars of religion offer every time I teach Introduction to Religion— namely, that religion is whatever is the most important thing in one's life. For Tillich, ultimate concern involves more than what is urgent or important at a particular moment in one's life. Rather, it is what gives one's life its ultimate meaningfulness. For a youth in Nazi Germany in the 1930s, it would not be a romance that could provide a sense of ultimacy, but Nazism did offer an ultimate seriousness, albeit demonic, in a culture lacking depth, according to Tillich.[36]

Of course, Tillich's notion of ultimate concern banks on an immediate point of identity between the human being and the divine, a mystical a priori.[37] Even when humans invest their ultimate concern in finite manifestations or conduits of the infinite, even mistakenly, even demonically, their awareness of ultimacy results from an immediate awareness of the ultimate reality, of the divine. That assumption stemming from Tillich's German Romantic Idealist heritage is no longer credible to many today. In

---

[35] Gary E. Kessler, *Studying Religion: An Introduction through Cases*, 3rd ed. (New York: McGraw-Hill, 2008) 21–22.

[36] Paul Tillich, *Theology of Culture,* ed. Robert C. Kimball (New York: Oxford University Press, 1959) 152.

[37] Paul Tillich, *Systematic Theology*, 3 vols. (Chicago: University of Chicago Press, 1951–1963) 1:9 and 1:44–45; *Dynamics of Faith* (New York: Harper & Row, 1957) 53, 70–71, and 83; and *Theology of Culture*, 10, 16, and 22–26.

light of this change in milieu, I will offer a reconstruction of the idea of ultimate concern in terms of human embodiment as outlined above.

Before beginning that constructive work, I must engage in a bit of "deconstruction" of Tillich's thought relative to embodiment. For the most part, Tillich's anthropology and ontology avoids dualism. He holds that the physical world does make a positive contribution to the divine life, a point made most explicitly in volume 3 of the *Systematic Theology*.[38] He affirms a continuity in the various types and levels of being in the universe. He denies that the self exists outside of the self-world correlation. Even in eternity, a finite creature's experience involves embodiment in some sense. Still, one might expect a touch of dualism to appear, given the idealistic component of his just-mentioned heritage. Tillich does appear to succumb to some split between thought and essence on the one hand and embodied existence on the other, as he endorses the following aspects of an Augustinian "ontological approach":

> These ultimate principles and knowledge of them are independent of the changes and relativities of the individual mind; they are the unchangeable, eternal light, appearing in the logical and mathematical axioms as well as in the first categories of thought. These principles are not created functions *of* our mind, but the presence of truth itself and there-

---

[38] Tillich, *Systematic Theology*, 3:398 and 3:422–23. I have argued, however, that the contribution that the world makes to divine fulfillment is independent of particular decisions by creatures. That is to say, God unfailingly supplements however much creatures' earthly actuality falls short of their essence in an eternal fulfillment. See David Nikkel, *Panentheism in Hartshorne and Tillich: A Creative Synthesis* (New York: Peter Lang, 1995) 177–86.

fore of God, *in* our mind.[39]

The perspective of radical embodiment by contrast insists that any and all thought arises from our embodiment and has meaning, makes sense, only in light of that embodiment. At least from the perspective of a finite creature, conception is literally utterly inconceivable apart from our embodied orientation to a world. It has no thoroughly or clearly independent status. All thought, all thinking, even the most abstract, is embodied thinking.

Turning to developing an embodied notion of ultimate concern, neuroscientist Antonio Damasio expounds upon background feelings of our body states. Normally tacit rather than attended to with full consciousness, these background feelings of our body states are, nonetheless, always actual. Damasio learns from patients lacking normal background feelings, namely, anosognosiacs (literally, "no knowledge of disease"), who are victims of left-side paralysis but with no immediate or functional knowledge of said paralysis. Anosognosiacs claim to feel fine: any knowledge of their paralysis is external and fleeting; they are emotionally flat and unconcerned about their future.[40] Damasio surmises that, incapable of normal body-state background feelings, they remember and report a now quite outdated image of their bodies.[41] Damasio goes on to hypothesize that such background feelings, such "primordial representations of the body," play an important role in consciousness, "provid(ing) a core for the neural representation of self."[42] Indeed, they bestow "the feeling of life itself, the sense of being

---

[39] Tillich, *Theology of Culture*, 13.

[40] Damasio, *Descartes' Error*, 62–63 and 153.

[41] Ibid., 154.

[42] Ibid., 235ff; see also Damasio, *Feeling of What Happens*, 110 and 285–87.

[alive]."[43]

This idea has been more recently echoed by Thompson, who describes "sentience as the feeling of being alive," enabling an organism "to feel the presence of one's body and the world."[44] Interestingly, Thompson finds a French philosopher from the late eighteenth through early nineteenth century, Maine de Biran, who contested Descartes' notion of consciousness as disembodied. Instead, de Biran contended we find the "feeling of existence (*le sentiment de l'existence*)" in the sentience of motile organisms, specifically "in the bodily experience of exercising effort in movement."[45]

Tempting as it might be to explore various theories about the roots of consciousness or sentience in relation to thematizing ultimate concern, for now I want to return to Damasio, who agrees that our bodies always exist in correlation with an environment, but who invokes background feelings in order to focus on what it is within an organism that enables consciousness. Damasio stipulates that emotions, which he categorizes as background, "primary," or "social," are never simply neutral.[46] He characterizes joy as the primary emotion associated with preserving and enhancing the self.[47]

Given Damasio's perspective on emotions, I submit that joy constitutes an intensification of normal animal background feelings of one's body, of the sense of being alive. That is to say, background feelings are normally positive, furnishing a positive emotional sense of integral bodily presence. Obviously, diseased states like anosognosia associated with an impaired sense of self can radi-

---

[43] Damasio, *Descartes' Error*, 150.

[44] Thompson, *Mind in Life*, 221.

[45] Ibid., 229.

[46] Antonio R. Damasio, *Looking for Spinoza: Joy, Sorrow, and the Feeling Brain* (New York: Harcourt Brace & Co., 2003) 43ff and 93.

[47] Ibid., 13–14.

cally compromise normal background feelings. Additionally, major injury or disease can compromise these feelings. For a couple of days following major surgery, the effects of the surgery and lingering anesthetic most definitely deprived me of my normal sense of being alive. Furthermore, and again obviously, experiences of physical and/or psychological suffering may overwhelm these background feelings such that one's overall affective state is negative. Still, that the background feelings of animals, including humans, are usually positive offers support for a basic and primordial goodness to life, which is affirmed by many religious traditions, especially those that valorize more than they denigrate the body.

As above, this integral bodily presence always exists in correlation with an environment. Our basic orientation to our environment always involves cognitive, aesthetic, and affective elements. Here the cognitive element concerns knowing where we are—spatially, temporally, socially, culturally. Usually, we succeed in knowing where we are rather than being confused about our basic orientation. The aesthetic element, crucial for animal and human meaning, tends to be overlooked or slighted. As suggested above, Johnson, drawing on Dewey and others, targets the qualitative aspects of experience involving perception, proprioception, kinesthesia, thinking, and feeling. In this sense, aesthetics refers to the beauty or goodness of any experience or situation (or negatively its ugliness or badness), with art constituting a heightened and more or less formalized case. In my own thinking, probably even before my attention was explicitly drawn to the centrality of embodiment, I resonated with the crucial nature of the aesthetic dimension. For, if in the final analysis, the experiences of life are not on the whole good or beautiful, knowledge may be a consolation, but only a small one. Similarly, if life were not fundamentally good, ethics would have a much-diminished role in human experience.

ULTIMATE CONCERN AND EMBODIMENT:
CRITICAL ISSUES

The inextricable aesthetic element of our orientation to our environment, then, is normally positive. We humans and other animals have evolved such that there is a fundamental fit in our organism-environment interactions; the normally positive aesthetic and positive affect of our bodily orientation constitutes part of this basic attunement to or consonance with our environment. The positive nature of our orientation to our environments offers further support for the primordial goodness of embodied life. In relation to the orientation of motile organisms to their environment, Gibson uses the term "ambient array." When it comes to particulars, our environments typically offer many opportunities or "affordances," to invoke Gibson again, for our more particular embodied aesthetic and affective meanings. Of course, our attempts to reach desired meanings may be thwarted, sometimes in terrible or tragic ways. But meaning is not something extrinsic to or alien from our embodiment in the world, but part and parcel of that embodiment. The correlation of human and other animal organisms to their environments entails a basic at-home-ness of sentient life on earth.[48]

Especially through the sense of our bodily integrity, the sense of being alive, produced by our background body feelings and the aesthetic and affective value of orientation to our environment, our

---

[48] Such an at-home-ness is a crucial, and well-documented, feature of biblical cosmogonies. For instance, it is reflected in Genesis 1 with God's seeing as "good" the animals created on the fifth and sixth days and with the creation of humankind in God's image, as well as with the creation in Genesis 2 of Adam, human being in Hebrew, literally meaning "earth being." Exploring the at-home-ness of the body in its environment as this intersects with ultimate concern and biblical cosmogonies is an area of Christian theological reflection that could be explored much further.

embodiment evokes an intuitive sense of the goodness of life, a positive sense of the meaningfulness and sacredness of life, an at-home-ness in our skins and world, or a feeling that we are in some sense "meant to be here." My "ultimate" claim, if you will pardon the pun, is that *this positive sense of bodily integrity and harmonious attunement to our environment entails and explains our sense of ultimate concern, rather than an immediate sense of the unconditional divine a la Tillich.* In our postmodern age—or whatever age this is—this intuitive sense of the sacredness of life and why anything about our lives finally matters offers a plausible account of our ultimate concern, unlike Tillich's mystical a priori. Now this sense of the goodness of embodied life may stimulate intuitions and ideas about whether a good ultimate reality stands behind, serves as the source of, this universe. But I fear Tillich's "ontological approach" can no longer convince many folks today and that we are left with an approach that in some sense is "cosmological" in Tillich's terminology: relying on our embodied human experience of this cosmos.

Indeed, I detect a dualism within Tillich's understanding of how the finite achieves awareness and knowledge of the infinite. Regarding Tillich's mystical a priori, an immediate awareness of the divine, Tillich commendably insists that we become aware of the infinite only through experience of particular finite realities. Even those mystics who may imagine they leave behind all finite reality in an absolute identity with the divine fail to notice that their experience substantively involves a tradition of embodied meditative practice.[49] While for Tillich, there is a *point* of immediate identity with the divine, it does not constitute the whole of the person's experience. Thus, on one level the necessity of our em-

---

[49] Tillich, *Theology of Culture*, 28; compare with Tillich, *Systematic Theology*, 1:140.

bodiment seems to be affirmed.

On the other hand, a strange disconnect exists between our immediate awareness of the divine and our finite embodiment that accompanies it. For the relation of the finite to the infinite ends up being incidental or idiosyncratic. This disconnect may be inevitable, given that the alleged immediate awareness is of that which transcends: it is prior to the subject-object distinction or the self-world correlation. In contrast, distinguishing self from others and the environment (even as one correlates with one's environment) enters on the ground floor of biological embodied consciousness. According to Tillich, our engagement with any finite reality can become the occasion for revelation or, in this context, for taking notice of the mystical a priori. Thus, whether a particular finite reality becomes the occasion for immediate awareness of the divine is rather idiosyncratic to the individual person and situation.

For instance, it is true that Tillich finds one general style of art more conducive to revelation, namely, an expressive style. However, its conduciveness stems from its bending or breaking of ordinary reality, in contrast to idealistic or naturalistic styles that tend to keep us locked into the finite. And therein lies an irony relative to particular embodiment: more than the goodness or beauty of a particular finite reality, it is the negation of the finite that serves as the trigger for immediate awareness of the divine. The upshot of Tillich's scheme is that the particularity of the intrinsic qualities of any finite reality in comparison to any other finite reality becomes incidental to the revelation. The finite reality, then, functions merely as an incidental trigger.[50] Tillich's own cel-

---

[50] A related issue exists in Tillich's corpus: Whether symbols—including language about God, since almost all of it is symbolic for Tillich—can actually provide knowledge about God. Sometimes out of concern for mystery and/or to avoid idolatry, Tillich indicates that symbols are neither

ebrated case of a mystical, ecstatic breakthrough while viewing Botticelli's "Madonna and Child with Singing Angels," related in "One Moment of Beauty,"[51] is illustrative. Tillich does refer to "the colors of the paint" and "the beauty its painter had envisioned so long ago."[52] Yet, the particular beauty of Tillich's bodily engagement with that piece of art in distinction from other instances of beauty is not what reveals the divine. Tillich's penultimate comment on his revelatory experience proves consistent with his idea of an incidental triggering: "I have seen greater [paintings] since then."[53]

We have seen one aspect of the disconnect arising between our finite embodiment and the mystical a priori, that from the side of the finite the triggering of immediate awareness is incidental to our embodiment. Another aspect of this disconnection focuses on the divine side, of what awareness we have of the divine nature. I will cut to the chase, then analyze the problem: the mystical a priori provides no specific information about the divine nature. It is a universal "awareness," the same for all human beings. It always lies in the background,[54] though sometimes a person may "notice it."[55] This "ontological" awareness does entail a cognitive dimension, constituted by a general awareness of the ground and abyss of being, the power of being, being-itself. And being-itself implies as

---

true nor false, but rather constructive or destructive. Other times Tillich implies or states that symbols do provide knowledge and that some have more truth than others. This tension is expounded upon in Nikkel, *Panentheism*, 13–18.

[51] Paul Tillich, *On Art and Architecture*, ed. John Dillenberger and Jane Dillenberger (New York: Crossroad, 1987) 234–35.

[52] Ibid., 235.

[53] Ibid.

[54] Tillich, *Theology of Culture*, 22–26; *Systematic Theology*, 1:44–45.

[55] Tillich, *Theology of Culture*, 14.

well truth-itself and beauty-itself.[56] This awareness involves an "absolute" or "unconditional certainty"[57] "whenever conscious attention is focused on it,"[58] which logically cannot be denied—though it can be doubted psychologically.[59]

Tillich also speaks of the immediate awareness of the divine in terms of "absolute faith" in the "God above God." As above, it involves no specific or "*special* content, yet it is not without content" [emphasis Tillich's].[60] When "the power of being is effective in us" through absolute faith and its "courage to be," we can take upon ourselves the anxiety of doubting every concrete meaning, including any concrete or specific meaning of the divine.[61] However, this immediate awareness and alleged certainty or absoluteness provide no knowledge of an analogy between the divine and the embodied finite, no knowledge about the relationship of the divine to the meaning of my embodied life. Any connection of the being, goodness, and beauty of my life to the specific being, goodness, and beauty of the divine takes us (down) into the realm of risk and uncertainty and into the cosmological approach to the divine.

Thus, despite Tillich's correct insistence that our total experience involving any awareness of the divine is not disembodied, the component or constituent of that total experience, which is awareness by the mystical a priori, strikes me as quite discarnate. A dualism obtains between the plane of mystical, ontological awareness of the divine and the plane of the meaning of our embodied existence vis-à-vis the divine. At this point, I have circled back to the

---

[56] Ibid., 15.

[57] Ibid., 15–16, and 23.

[58] Ibid., 23.

[59] Ibid., 13.

[60] Paul Tillich, *The Courage to Be* (New Haven CT: Yale University Press, 1952) 182.

[61] Ibid., 181–89.

untenability of the "ontological approach" and the mystical a priori. Instead, we need a revalorized "cosmological approach" in which our embodied experience may tell us something ultimate about the nature of reality.

For Tillich, ultimate concern involves a basis for judging the adequacy of religions, including secular culture insofar as it manifests ultimate concern. The only rightful recipient of that ultimate concern, the divine depth and ground of being, constitutes that basis. A finite reality that claims ultimacy for itself is thus idolatrous and even demonic. Can my refashioning of ultimate concern provide any basis for judging the adequacy of religions? As I have stated, an important aspect of this sense of ultimate concern involves our basic biological orientation to our environment. For human beings, with our reflective, linguistic, and artistic capabilities, this pre-reflective ultimate concern can find expression in attempts to orient ourselves to the largest worlds of meaning we can imagine. Reflection on the intuitive sense of the sacredness of one's embodied life in the world should rather obviously lead to respect for every life as sacred and to ecological concern for the environment that enables and sustains life. Of course, my sense of ultimate concern entails a primordial sense of the goodness of life in the body—of the background feelings of our bodily integrity and of our embodied orientation to our ambience. Such attempts to orient ourselves may provide the basis for a normative theory about the nature of religion, even as Tillich's concept of ultimate concern grounded his theory of religion. Therefore, a theory based on this notion of ultimate concern would judge as deficient religious beliefs that deny the ultimate significance of the body and embodiment. It would also call them on importing notions of embodiment even as they deny the body. For, from the perspective of our radical embodiment, whatever visions of life or afterlife or mystical experience they conjure that attempt to escape the body must necessarily invoke bodily images to have any meaning—in order to be understood or to have any value for us at all. Abandonment of the certainty of the mystical a priori may invoke even greater respect for the ultimate mystery of existence than Tillich's system allows. Even so, the sense of the primordial goodness of our embodiment as ultimately concerning us may invite the inference of a good source of the environment in which "we live and move and have our being" and imaginative thought about the nature of that ultimate source.

2

Multiplicity and Ultimate Concern(s)

KAYKO DRIEDGER HESSLEIN

When presenting the body as a site of universal experience, Tillich's use of the representative category of "the body" erases the individual body. The universalizing nature of his concept of "ultimacy" too easily determines the existence of the particular in a totalizing manner that discards the uniqueness of bodies in favor of categorical assimilation, caused in part by his use of abstract and generalizing language that discounts particularities. In Tillich's system, there is an overcoming of the finite by the infinite: all is made subject to the absolute. As will become clear, this complete subjection stands in need of correction in order for the body, which is unique in essence, to continue functioning.

As we seek to understand the relationship between a common universal concern, as it is located in the body, and the individuals that make up the broader category of "human body," Laurel Schneider's insistence on differentiating between the individual body and the generalized human body is integral. She provides a critical corrective to Tillich's approach that re-centers work on theology and the body today. Schneider argues that individuals cannot be reduced to categories: this removes their individuality, and denies their unique irreducibility and irreplaceability. Individual bodies share the fact of existing in human contingencies, but not the details. It is the details, however, that form an individual body's existence in the world, not the general categories by which they are described.

Applying Schneider's observations to Tillich, I argue that treating the generalized category of "the body" as a site of resolution for humankind's ultimate concern obscures the particularities of individual human existence. The singular body is replaced by a representative status, and is segregated as a "universal human" from one's irreplaceable network of formative relationships, in the same ways that the moniker of "citizen" obscures the diversity and uniqueness of participation of each individual in the formation of their country. In this process, one's identity as a human body is entirely defined through generalizations. Just as individuals cease to become individuals when the particularities of their historical contingencies are relativized or expunged, a singular human body also loses its individuality.

TILLICH'S SINGULAR ULTIMATE CONCERN

Tillich's theology of "ultimate concern," and his approach to the human condition and its response to this ultimate concern are rooted in his correlative, or rather paradoxical, approach. This is, in large part, due to Tillich's insistence on "reason" or rational thinking as the basis for his theological method. Rejecting bodily-based theologies, or those that focus primarily on experience as the foundation for theological inquiry, he turns to rational thinking. "Reason," he says, "is the structure of the mind which enables the mind to grasp and transform reality."[1] As a result, the theologian "discusses causality in relation to a *prima causa*, the ground of the whole series of causes and effects."[2] Tillich, therefore, structures

---

[1] Paul Tillich, *Systematic Theology*, 3 vols. (Chicago: University of Chicago Press, 1951–1963) 1:72.

[2] Tillich, *Systematic Theology*, 1:24.

his entire theological system, with its culmination in ultimate concern, on a singular cause that is at the root of all things and is its goal.

Yet, the multiplicity that exists in our lives, and in the poles of our lives, confronts Tillich, and so he refers to the paradoxical existence of the human self. He gives us, for example, the paradoxes/polarities of individualization and participation, dynamism and form, and freedom and destiny, each exhibiting a tension between particularity and universality. Within these polarized sets, Tillich argues that the interrelation of both poles constitutes the ontological self. He cautions that when the first term of a given polarity becomes dominant, we become overdetermined by particularity and Tillich's specific sense of finitude—an inevitable determination given our historical existence—and a disruptive imbalance comes to pervade the respective polarities. Likewise, if the second term of each polarity becomes dominant, we are overdetermined by universality and Tillich's specific sense of infinitude, becoming the faceless self that loses her irreplaceability, which is Schneider's concern.

Tillich's *Systematic Theology* emphasizes a concern for the dominance of the first term in each pair, a concern with overdetermination by particularity that becomes an obstacle for those who understand multiplicity as integral to bodies. As will be seen in more depth, bodies can be understood as constituted of multiple, even paradoxical, attributes. Bodies have traditionally been viewed as sites of singularity, or purity, where differences are reconciled into a homogeneous unity; however, recent work on the body has argued that difference and multiplicity are essential to bodies. Tillich's paradox-based model, following traditional emphases on singularity and purity, leads him to view multiplicity as a mutual exclusivity that leads ultimately to destructive conflict.

Thus, for Tillich, multiple particularities existing within one body are undesirable impossibilities as the particular is inevitably set against every other particular.[3] Indeed, his chief objection to particularity as the basis for Logos or the New Being of Christ is that "particularity excludes every particular from every other one."[4] Tillich's concreteness, as differentiated from particularity, includes other concrete differences, yet particularity does not. The human being, as existence in history, is undeniably limited by the particularity and finitude of the individual.[5] Tillich admits no possibility that a particular human individual can exist other than in a conflictual relationship with another individual in his or her own particularity.

Indeed, Tillich argues that this conflict-determined particularity of the self is a constituent aspect of the human self. As individuals, we are connected with those around us—Tillich is no isolationist—but the conflict with the Other is a necessary limitation to the self, one that prevents us from what he considers our inevitable tendency to make our particularity universal. As he says, "If [a self] did not meet the resistance of other selves, every self would try to make himself absolute. But the resistance of the other selves is unconditional. ...The individual discovers himself through this resistance. ...In the resistance of the other person, the person is born. Therefore, there is no person without an encounter with other persons."[6] While Tillich goes on to say that "persons can grow only in the communion of personal encounter" (and I will return to the hope that this statement offers for multiply-identifying or multiply-particular bodies), this encounter becomes

---

[3] Tillich, *Systematic Theology*, 1:17.
[4] Tillich, *Systematic Theology*, 1:17, fn.5.
[5] Tillich, *Systematic Theology*, 1:152.
[6] Tillich, *Systematic Theology*, 1:176–77.

one that, for Tillich, is necessarily rooted in conflict.[7]

Tillich understands this conflict to resolve only through a sacrifice of the particular to the greater unity. Indeed, we are aware that the New Being is the One who has sacrificed the particularities of his historical existence to the Spirit, as "everything finite in him, from his special traditions, from his individual piety, form his rather conditioned worldview."[8] Insofar as all humans are moved towards the same existence as the New Being, all humans are also in the position of needing to sacrifice their particularities (plural) to the larger, and united, ultimate. Because particularities yearn towards becoming totalities, which would erase other particularities, they must be sacrificed through transcendence to the "absolutely concrete."[9]

Tillich's argument becomes somewhat circular at this point: particularity tends towards totality because all things tend towards a totality based on the singularity of any given particularity; therefore, particularities must be resisted. Yet, resisting particularities by sacrificing them to the absolute or ultimate *transcendental* only reinforces the biases against multiplicity.[10] He rules out mutually-constituting particularities because they cannot exist, and they do not exist in his worldview because he has already sacrificed them as a logical impossibility. Caught in a Catch-22 of his own making, Tillich must argue that the necessarily conflictual relationships of differences preclude the possibility of a multiply-particular individual. His approach to polytheism, in fact, captures this perfectly vis-à-vis multiply-religious bodies, when he says that polytheism "is not a belief in a plurality of gods but rather the lack of a uniting

---

[7] Tillich, *Systematic Theology*.
[8] Tillich, *Systematic Theology*, 1:134.
[9] Tillich, *Systematic Theology*, 1:16.
[10] Tillich, *Systematic Theology*, 2:11.

and transcending ultimate which determines its characters. Each of the polytheistic divine powers claims ultimacy in the concrete situation in which it appears. …This leads to conflicting claims and threatens to disrupt the unity of self and the world."[11] Tillich interprets plural beliefs in one believer—or one body—as plural claims to an ultimacy, claims that can only ever be mutually exclusive.

MULTIPLE BODIES

I now turn to the challenge that Tillich's notion of ultimate concern poses for bodies constituted by multiplicity. Ultimate concern correlates to the anxiety of our finite existence, transcending the finite and the particular. Due to the ultimacy of ultimate concern, these elements of finitude and particularity must yield to unity. Bodies constructed in terms of multiple particulars cannot exist in such a model. The elements of our finite existence, in which the multiple facets of our particularity come to light, are precisely what ultimate concern is meant to transcend. Tillich's concept does not allow for the existence of those individuals for whom multiple particulars constitute the united self and in whom the particulars exist for the mutual building-up of each, rather than mutual destruction.

In the process of emphasizing the general, representational status of one particular body as the New Being, Tillich sets aside the actual particulars of that (and every) body's historical life. I follow Schneider in arguing that the particularities of historical existence constitute bodies as singular participants in the flow of time. Furthermore, bodies are existences shaped by the multiple relationships in which humans engage. The unique combination

---

[11] Tillich, *Systematic Theology*, 1:222.

of these relationships forms each individual such that no single human body can stand in for another, what Schneider identifies as "irreplaceable." Thus, the existence of these multiply-constituted bodies in all their unique-nesses disrupts the very category of "*the*" body and the universality of the ultimate concern of every body.

Tillich flees from this idea. Instead, he relies on his presupposition that multiple-formativity of an individual is not possible, as he argues that the historical particularity of a body cannot be formative of his or her concrete existence. The multiplicity of particularity is something to be overcome through concreteness. Today, it hardly seems possible to continue following Tillich in his logic to this point if we take seriously the experiences of multiply-constituted bodies.

Multiply-constituted bodies have been the subject of theorization by those working in the field of multiculturalism. Rita Dhamoon proposes that the multiple particularities of one individual do not function in an "additive" manner, whereby characteristics add up to a multiply-hyphenated description of an individual, but rather multiple particularities are interdependent, existing in a matrix, creating an integrated person through a process more akin to multiplication than addition.[12] Laurel Schneider also points to the constitutive, rather than combative, nature of differences, arguing that individuality arises because of our individual combinations of unique and even contradictory particularities.[13] Applying Schneider's observations to Tillich, I argue that treating the broad category of "the body" as a site of resolution for human-

---

[12] Rita Dhamoon, *Identity/Difference Politics: How Difference Is Produced and Why It Matters* (Vancouver: University of British Columbia Press, 2009) 35.

[13] Laurel Schneider, *Beyond Monotheism: A Theology of Multiplicity* (London: Routledge, 2008) 165.

kind's ultimate concern obscures the particularities of individual human existence. The singular body is replaced by a representative status, and is segregated as a "universal human" from one's irreplaceable network of formative relationships. This is analogous to the way the moniker of "citizen" obscures the diversity and uniqueness of each individual's participation in the formation of their country. In this process, one's bodily identity becomes defined entirely through a generically human characterization. Just as individuals cease to become individuals when the particularities of their historical contingencies are relativized or expunged, a singular human body also loses its individuality, along with its multiplicity.

Toni Erskine, operating in the field of international relations, illustrates this clearly. She proposes that individuals participate in "overlapping memberships" in various communities. As a member of one community, an individual forms and is formed by the relationships within that community and with the community as a whole. As a participant in several communities, these multiple relationships and formations overlap without causing the disintegration that Tillich fears. Indeed, within the one individual, these memberships continue to accumulate and interrelate, bringing a new reality and a new self into being. Here, Tillich's supposedly conflicted particularities exist without conflict. Rather, the intersections of multiple particularities are life-giving. The existence of bodies constituted by multiple particularities thus derails Tillich's argument that particularities must always come into conflict. In doing so, they further disrupt Tillich's proposal for a singular ultimate concern that transcends every particularity.

MULTIPLY-RELIGIOUS BODIES

Although many groups of individuals participate in this disruption, one stands out in particular. Multiply-religious, or multifaith, bodies challenge Tillich's singular ultimate concern in a significant way. The numbers of individuals who identify with more than one faith in a substantial and practice-based way are increasing. These multi-faith bodies are not merely theoretical. Twenty-four percent of Americans say they regularly or occasionally attend services of a religion other than their own, according to a 2009 Pew Report. Of those who attend a weekly religious service, almost 30 percent have attended services outside of their own faith.[14] Forty percent of marriages today are interfaith, and as of 2008, 37 percent of families identified as such.[15] The Interfaith Families Project, an organization in Washington, D.C., that offers religious services and "school" specifically for interfaith families registers 300 active members. The Chicago Interfaith Family School registers over 70 families.[16] In both places, children who have grown up in practicing interfaith families, in which both religions are maintained, or who are currently growing up with these multiple practices, describe themselves as "both." They shun the half-and-half nomenclature, which would fit within the paradoxical or polarity-based structure of Tillich's work, opting instead for more integrative, "fully-both," language.

---

[14] "Many Americans Mix Multiple Faiths" (Washington, D.C.: Pew Research Center, December 9, 2009) http://www.pewforum.org/2009/12/09/ many-americans-mix-multiple-faiths/.

[15] Stephanie Haynes, "Interfaith America: 'Being both' is a rising trend in the US," *The Christian Science Monitor*, November 23, 2014, http://www.csmonitor.com/The-Culture/Family/2014/1123/Interfaith-America-Being-both-is-a-rising-trend-in-the-US Last.

[16] "The Family School," The Interfaith Family School, Chicago, IL, accessed February 7, 2016, http://the-family-school.org/.

It is important to understand the level at which these individuals view their religions as embodied, not just intellectually adopted phenomena. In other words, their multiply-religious lives contribute to the ontological constructions of the self, particularly through the rituals they participate in, as will be seen below. While theologians like Peter Phan deny the possibility of any true multiply-religious existence, those who live this existence argue for the fullness of both religions in their lives.[17] Karla Suomola argues, "In their attempt to grasp the complexity of religious identity, the theological terms…largely fail to communicate the very dynamic, fluid, thick, relational nature of religious identity," and, I would add, the embodied and constitutive nature of religious identity.[18]

Individuals who live multiply-religious lives describe themselves as living as "both" in an embodied way that, though paradoxical, feels whole in themselves. Susan Katz Miller explores their descriptions in her research on children who have been raised in interfaith programs.[19] These programs intentionally support multiple-faith identities, and the children whose families attend them are just now reaching adulthood. They say things like, "I want to stay both, because it's original and it represents part of who I am." Another says, "I feel the coupling of both faiths has given me unique avenues to God." And another says, "I cannot be severed from either of these religions, nor be limited to [either alone]."

The theme of being both, and not half, resonates with many

---

[17] Peter Phan, "Multiple Religious Belonging: Opportunities and Challenges for Theology and Church," *Theological Studies* 64/3 (Fall 2003): 496–97.

[18] Karla R. Suomala, "Complex religious identity in the context of interfaith dialogue," *Cross Currents* 62/3 (September 2012): 360–70.

[19] Susan Katz Miller, *On Being Both: Embracing Two Religions in One Interfaith Family* (Boston: Beacon Press, 2013) 179, 181, and 182.

raised in multi-faith families. When asked if he is half-Jew and half-Christian, for example, one person Katz interviews responds, "No, because I don't think you can be half a religion. I say I'm both. I don't think I can ever say I was ever confused about what I was, because I always just kind of understood that I was both." Testifying to the embodied nature of being both, another person, when pushed to identify with only one faith, responded, "I'm actually inter-faith. I was raised Christian and Jewish. So, for me to pick one over the other and say I'm just Jewish, it's kind of like asking me to pick if I'm white or Latino."[20]

Amongst these interfaith children-become-adults, 90 percent of them stated that belonging to two faiths was complex, but not confusing, and indeed life-giving. Believing in *mitzvot* and *tzedekah* as foundational for Jewish ethics contributes to the Christian understanding of Jesus' call to care for the poor and love your neighbor as yourself. Believing in the second coming of Christ as a time when God's peace will reign deepens the Jewish understanding of *tikkun olam* and the healing of the world.

Rituals are one way in which beliefs become embodied, and come to constitute the self as the body of the self performs the ritual. Participating in the Passover rite of the Seder—with its actions of reading aloud, eating, dipping, raising a glass, tasting when performed within the Christian Holy Week, as it normally is—works with the embodied-ness of Holy Communion on Easter Sunday: of eating, tasting, speaking aloud, raising a glass. Both rites deepen within one another as they give rise to a fuller thanksgiving, the goal of both Seder and Communion. The embodied act of lighting the candles every Sunday in Advent works with the act of lighting the Hanukkah candles for eight consecutive nights,

---

[20] Ibid., 194.

deepening the meaning of bringing light into the world in times of great darkness. Those male children who were born into actively Jewish-Christian interfaith families experience within their own bodies the covenant of circumcision of the Jewish people and the covenant of baptism of the Christian people. The covenants do not preclude each other, but serve to construct the meaning of the other more deeply. Circumcision physically marks the covenants in a way that baptism lacks, while baptism, as it leads to communion, moves the covenant internally, week after week in the taking in of the bread and wine of the Christian Eucharist. In other words, there is no paradox that leads to conflict or the sacrifice of one to the other.[21] Instead, the paradox exists so that one difference contributes to the other difference, and vice versa, in a mutually constructive way.

DEPTH AS CAPACITY FOR MULTIPLE PARTICULARITY

To accommodate this lived and embodied paradox, we must set aside Tillich's point that the finite particular must sacrifice itself to the infinite universal (a sacrifice that I note is only one-way). Tillich's theology would probably not withstand this bracketing, yet we might creatively build on Tillich's development of paradox by emphasizing how paradoxical tension can become a source of construction rather than a source of conflict. To do this, I draw on Tillich's vision of God as personal and Christ as concrete, and on his understanding of the poles of individualization and participation in the human community.

Tillich argues that only a personal God can bring together concreteness with the ultimate. "The God of Israel is a concrete God," he says.[22] A personal God is needed because a non-personal

---

[21] Tillich, *Systematic Theology*, 1:198.
[22] Ibid., 1:227

God can only be ultimate and never concrete, thus disrupting the necessary paradox between concrete and ultimate that defines the human condition. In the New Being, Jesus as the Christ becomes "the bearer of all that which is absolute without condition and restriction," as well as having, as a human, "the most concrete of all possible forms of concreteness."[23] For Tillich, the divine life allows the concrete and universal aspects of human existence to be "without tension and without dissolution for God is being-itself."[24] To manifest in Jesus the Christ, the New Being "must represent everything particular and must be the point of identity between the absolutely concrete and the absolutely universal. Insofar as he is absolutely universal, the relation to him includes potentially all possible relations and can, therefore, be unconditional and infinite."[25]

If we set aside Tillich's argument that the New Being accomplishes this by sacrificing his own unique particularity to this universal concreteness, we see here the possibility for multiple identities to exist within one person in a way that is inclusive—as multiple concretions, rather than exclusive—as multiple particularities. Tillich allows for this potential, though he constrains its realization to the divine. Here, I am arguing for a broader anthropology that extends the capacity for multiplicity to humans.

Insofar as Tillich can envision polarities to exist without tension, and as contributing to or even constituting the nature of being itself (not Being-itself), we can conceive of the human being as one in whom polarities or multiply-particular identities constitute being-ness. Tillich offers a window through which we might see being-ness finding its existence in infinite variations and uncondi-

---

[23] Ibid., 1:150.
[24] Ibid., 1:243.
[25] Ibid., 1:17.

53

tional relationships, rather than in mutually exclusive tensions and anxieties that are only resolved through sacrificing one aspect of particularity to another. Through this window, we can see that embodied participations in multiple communities, even religious communities with beliefs based on irreplaceable and totalizing particularities, can overlap one another in an individual. The individual who is embodied in and embodies these multiple particularities increases the respective essentialness of each particularity embodied. Within the human individual's capacity for absolute concreteness as a particularity that relates to all other particularities (a capacity that, to be sure, Tillich does not accept as existing), we might then explain the multiple particularities that exist without demanding the sacrifice of one to the other. This is not so much an abandonment of Tillich's desire to uncover a universal that characterizes the human condition, but a revision of it. The universal is one's particularity as it is constituted by multiple particularities.

Although we turn away here from Tillich's ultimate concern, his use of the polarity of individualization and participation offers a more productive way to engage his thought vis-à-vis the lived realities of multiply-religious bodies. Tillich proposes that a human who is properly individualized is also properly self-centered. This self-centeredness is "constitutive of every being" such that the self-centered being does not experience any division at its core: there is no fragmentation or splitting apart of the particularities that constitute its particular existence.[26] Indeed, Tillich even uses the word "manifoldness" to describe the complexity that the self engages when it is integrated enough to move between its center and its periphery.[27] Given Tillich's use of this concept in volume

---

[26] Ibid., 1:176.
[27] Ibid., 3:33.

three of his *Systematic Theology*, as well as his subsequent change of heart following his extended time in Japan in 1960, one wonders whether he himself might have, in due time, also considered multiply-religious bodies.[28] Apart from such speculation regarding Tillich's later writings, this undivided center of the self offers space to claim that identifying with multiple religious identities creates a more complex self, rather than leading to a divided and anxious self who cannot decide between two religions and who will ultimately be torn apart, as many critics of interfaith families argue.

Tillich balances individualization with participation, with the latter being the means by which we avoid fracturing the world into a million different individuals.[29] Participation entails relationship, and the relational existence between the "self and the world is the basic ontological structure and implies all the others."[30] In his inclusive, universal soteriology he argues that a person cannot be separated from another person such that only one is saved while the others are not.[31] Furthermore, on a more constitutive level, he argues that "the person as the fully developed individual self is impossible without other fully developed selves. …Persons can grow only in the communion of personal encounter."[32]

Tillich sees the constitutive encounter as taking place between different persons, but there is room to see the encounter as taking place within one person as well. That is, a person with multiple religious identities finds his or her self as it is formed by one religious community encountering the same self as it is formed by

---

[28] For further development on this idea, see Tomoaki Fukai and Friedrich Wilhelm Graf, eds., *Paul Tillich—Journey to Japan in 1960* (Berlin; Boston: De Gruyter, 2013).

[29] Tillich, *Systematic Theology*, 1:177.

[30] Ibid., 1:171.

[31] Ibid., 1:147.

[32] Ibid., 1:176.

another religious community. Erskine's account of overlapping memberships is a model where the overlap and encounter occur within the singular individual. The relationships of the self to one religious community encounter the relationships of the same self to another religious community, thereby constituting an internal or singularly embodied communion of difference. This communion of difference deepens the individual body's participation *and* one's individualization. The integrative possibilities of mutually constitutive or mutually enriching particularities that Tillich assumes to be impossible in actuality contribute to Tillich's own aim of realizing a more "fully developed self."[33] In this model, however, it occurs through the polarity of individualization and participation.

Theologically, this work requires a movement from understanding the body in terms of the phenomenological experience of ultimate concern to understanding the body—particularly the multiply-religious body—as a site where multiple ultimate concerns overlap and encounter one another. The body, as a mutually formative participant with other bodily existences, dismantles the universalizing tendencies of a singular ultimate concern while simultaneously opening conversation towards the construction of a theological anthropology that sees the particular body and the universal body as mutually formative and multiply-relational realities. Tillich's polarities are jeopardized if we set aside the sacrificial component, however. Tillich's emphasis on the sacrifice of the particular to the absolute does not immediately make room for the self to develop or deepen in the ways that I propose. Tillich's insistence that the particular tends towards universalization in a way that excludes other particularities keeps any door to multiply-

---

[33] Ibid.

identified selves firmly shut, as does any theology that privileges a universalization based on abstraction or generalization as the starting point for characterizing the human body. What I have proposed, therefore, are windows for new glimpses, rather than doors we can walk through, as I look to build a universal constituted by particularity. However, while my proposal requires abandoning Tillich's *a priori* acceptance of united singularity as the beginning and end of ontological development, Tillich's method of correlation, pursued by other authors in this volume, encourages alternate questions—and answers—to be generative for new bodies.

3

Stress Eating
Anxiety, Hunger, and Courageous Love

BETH RITTER-CONN

Throughout the epistles, the apostle Paul makes it clear that eating is not a personal matter. It does not merely affect an individual body. For Paul, the way one ate was an expression of the way one loved: "If your brother or sister is being injured by what you eat, you are no longer walking in love" (Rom. 14:15a).

In the early churches—particularly, it seems from the epistles, in Rome and Corinth—different understandings of the morality of eating meat created a point of this potential "injury." For Jewish Christians in predominantly Gentile communities, one concern would have been that most meat had not been prepared according to the dietary laws outlined in the Torah. Another concern was whether it was acceptable to eat meat that had been sacrificed to idols; most of the meat available for consumption in the public market would have been sacrificed to "pagan" deities, or at least would have been sold in the temples of these other gods. Moreover, eating meat was itself a privilege due to its expense. The discomfort some Christians would have felt, at least in the Corinthian community, and likely also in the Roman churches, about church members eating the sacrificed meat may have been layered on top of the inequality it represented; it was inaccessible to all but a wealthy few in the first place, or could be purchased only rarely on special occasions.[1] Paul tells the church that there is nothing inherently wrong with eating meat; he emphasizes that those who choose to eat meat should not judge those who do not, and vice versa. The comments Paul makes about church members eating together are part of his exhortations on the nature and limits of freedom within a culturally and socioeconomically diverse community that is supposed to be characterized chiefly by love and faith.[2]

Though the particulars of what it might mean to eat lovingly are different today, the spirit of Paul's exhortation is freshly relevant, as he draws attention to the dynamics of privilege, inclusion, and exclusion—love and harm—that can be expressed through the way we eat.

Today, our food systems are so globally diffuse that those who grow and prepare food for most of the world remain anonymous and invisible to those of us in the so-called "First World," and the methods by which our food is grown and processed are wreaking ecological havoc on this planet we share. Our own over-

---

[1] I am grateful to my friend and colleague Amanda Miller, a scholar of Greek who teased out the particulars of this passage for me and helped me understand the kind of "injury" Paul intends in Romans 14:15, here and elsewhere in this chapter. I also thank Kyle Butler, who read and gave invaluable feedback on early drafts of this chapter. Finally, I would like to express gratitude to Adam Pryor, an outstanding editor and even better friend, who repeatedly understood and named what I was trying to say when I could not find the words. Any error in what follows is entirely my own.

[2] See N.T. Wright, "The Letter to the Romans," in *The New Interpreter's Bible: A Commentary in Twelve Volumes, Volume X* (Nashville: Abingdon Press, 2002) esp. 740–41; Leander E. Keck, *Abingdon New Testament Commentaries: Romans* (Nashville: Abingdon Press, 2005); Richard A. Horsley, *Abingdon New Testament Commentaries: 1 Corinthians* (Nashville: Abingdon Press, 1998); J. Paul Sampley, "The First Letter to the Corinthians," in *The New Interpreter's Bible: A Commentary in Twelve Volumes, Volume X* (Nashville: Abingdon Press, 2002) 899–902.

consumption is also directly tied to others' starvation: 40 percent of the food in the U.S. food system goes into landfills every year, while one in seven people in this country do not have enough to eat. In short, there is a profound disconnect between where food comes from, how it gets eaten, and who gets to eat it. To borrow Paul's language, many of our "brothers and sisters," both locally and globally, are being "injured" by how privileged bodies choose to eat.

The perception of scarcity coupled with the very real issue of food insecurity gives rise to a complex web of anxieties surrounding food. Anxiety is bodily. It weighs us down. It stirs up our stomachs. It causes us to hold tension in places where we did not even know we had muscles to tense. Any theology that attempts to address the anxiety of being alive must address it as something that affects our flesh. Another Paul—Paul Tillich—provides us with language to consider anxiety theologically. It is a condition of being alive that gives rise to questions calling for theological responses.

Tillich teaches us that the response to the estrangement that arises from anxiety is courageous love that reconnects us to one another and to the ground of being. Here, I will address one symptom of estrangement and anxiety that we experience today—food insecurity and the precarity of the lives of the people who experience it—and envision a response rooted in the expansive, courageous love that Tillich recommends. However, I want to experiment with a shift in Tillich's ideas: identifying potential *non*-being as the basis of connection and solidarity. Rather than isolating and insulating us from one another, can the recognition of our vulnerability to non-being instead ground the connections among us and dismantle the walls of estrangement? The anxiety that comes from being in a body is an expression of anxiety over being vulnerable—to death, to need, to one another. And the pervasive Western myth that each of us is an autonomous individual only exacerbates that anxiety, because it stands in contrast to what we *know* in our bodies: we are dependent creatures.

ANXIETY THEN AND NOW

Ever the keen observer of the human condition, Tillich noted early in his career that to be alive is to experience anxiety. He defines anxiety as the response each of us has to an awareness of our finitude; it is "the state in which a being is aware of its possible non-being."[3] Tillich's awareness of this aspect of human existence was personal. As a military chaplain during World War I, he experienced what he called "the shock of non-being," the phenomenon of being confronted with the precariousness of his own life and the urgent reality of his mortality.

Still, this shock of non-being was not his alone. As he observes in *The Courage to Be*, "Today it has become almost a truism to call our time an 'age of anxiety.' This holds equally true for America and Europe."[4] In a century steeped in war (and in Freudian psychoanalysis that popularized the extent of subconscious anxiety), Tillich's diagnosis certainly would have rung true in Western Europe and North America. The invincibility and optimism that had characterized the Golden Age of the late nineteenth century had given way to a century of violent war that seemed senseless, the dissolution of ostensibly sovereign states, and a feeling of despair in the face of these swift shifts. Theology that emerged from the West during this era, including Tillich's, responded to the

---

[3] Paul Tillich, *The Courage to Be*, 3rd ed. (New Haven: Yale University Press, 2014 [1952]) 34; see also his *Systematic Theology*, 3 vols. (Chicago: University of Chicago Press, 1951–1963) 1:64.

[4] Tillich, *The Courage to Be*, 34.

sense of disorientation that these changes birthed.

Today, Tillich's observations regarding personal and social anxiety still resonate. Scott Stossel, in his book *My Age of Anxiety* (a play on W.H. Auden's 1947 poem *The Age of Anxiety*), notes the precipitous rise in diagnoses and treatment of anxiety disorders in recent years—as measured by the number of prescriptions for medications like Xanax, Ativan, and other drugs used to treat clinical anxiety. This correlates with physician-reported anecdotal evidence that "anxiety is one of the most frequent complaints driving patients to their offices—more frequent, by some accounts, than the common cold."[5] Anxiety diagnoses (and related conditions) spike in particular after nationally and internationally distressing crises. "In the weeks after 9/11," Stossel notes, "Xanax prescriptions jumped 9 percent nationally—and by 22 percent in New York City."[6] A similar trend occurred at the beginning of the economic depression in 2008.[7] Perhaps this can frame a recurring national crisis: college admissions. Students entering college today report more serious mental-health issues stemming from anxiety and depression every year.[8]

---

[5] Scott Stossel, *My Age of Anxiety: Fear, Hope, Dread, and the Search for Peace of Mind* (New York: Alfred A. Knopf, 2013) 9. This phenomenon is relatively new: anxiety did not become an officially diagnosable clinical condition until just under forty years ago—right around the time the drugs to treat it were developed (10).

[6] Here he cites Karen Springen, "Drugs: Taking the Worry Cure," *Newsweek,* 24 February 2003 <http://www.newsweek.com/drugs-taking-worry-cure-140223> Accessed 2 August 2016.

[7] Stossel, *My Age of Anxiety,* 9.

[8] This has been steadily increasing for at least the past six years. See the Penn State Center for Collegiate Mental Health (CCMH) Annual Report 2016: "…[A]nxiety and depression are not only the most common concerns, but students' distress in these areas appears to be growing slowly while other areas of distress are flat or decreasing" (1). <https://sites.psu.edu/ccmh/files/2017/01/2016-Annual-Report-FINAL_2016_01_09-1gc2hj6.pdf>

In what may be an echo of the anxiety expressed by sovereign colonizing nations coming to terms with their loss of power and recognition of their fallibility (initially revealed during Tillich's time), both the U.S. and Europe have seen a rise in nationalism and nativism—exemplified in phenomena like Brexit and the election of Donald Trump (in spite of his blatantly xenophobic rhetoric)—in the wake of generalized "election anxiety" that emerged across the political spectrum. Tillich would likely identify these specific phenomena (like Brexit or the 2016 U.S. presidential election) in terms of the tendency to transform anxiety into fear: the threat of non-being is transformed into the (often baseless) fear of concrete others, in these cases, fear of immigrants.

Not to be condoned, the transformation of anxiety to fear nevertheless has its own sort of logic; as Tillich puts it, "Anxiety strives to become fear, because fear can be met by courage."[9] While for the white majority a description in terms of fear may be accurate, for racial, ethnic, and gender minorities these events heighten anxiety over how future well-being can be sought in such hostile environments. One group's fear leads to another group's anxiety.

The distinction between fear and anxiety mirrors the wider distinction Tillich makes between the things that threaten our *existence* and the things that threaten our *being*. He says,

> Nothing can be of ultimate concern for us which does not have the power of threatening and saving our being. The term "being" in this context does not designate existence in time and space. Existence is continuously threatened and saved by things and events which have no ultimate concern for us. But the term "being" means the whole of human reali-

---

[9] Tillich, *The Courage to Be*, 37.

ty, the structure, the meaning, and the aim of existence.[10]

Food insecurity and our eating habits might be taken as "fears" that threaten our existence on Tillich's account but not threats to our being. In what follows, I will more thoroughly make the case that food is intimately connected to our total being and is not just an element of our existence. For now, it is crucial to note that analyzing anxiety and its relation to fear is a complex task that is by no means easily accomplished.[11]

Regardless of how we divide distinctions between anxiety and fear, this twenty-first-century Western distress seems to originate from the same impulses as the anxiety of Tillich's time. As Tillich saw it, the anxiety we experience is closely tied to estrangement: estrangement "from the ground of [our] being, from other beings, and from [ourselves]" that causes us to question the meaningfulness of our existence.[12] By his account, this is a common human experience; the risk to our sense of self posed by anxiety presents an existential question that requires a theological response. Thus, in the face of this anxiety and estrangement, we seek "something—anything—that will help [us] avoid facing the precariousness of [our] own being."[13] While this search may seem like a quest for distraction at times, it is almost certainly rooted in a des-

---

[10] Tillich, *Systematic Theology*, 1:14.

[11] It is unclear, though, whether anxiety has intensified in our age or if we are simply increasingly aware of it. See Daniel Smith, "It's Still the 'Age of Anxiety.' Or Is It?" *New York Times*, 12 January 2012. Online edition. <http://opinionator.blogs.nytimes.com/2012/01/14/its-still-the-age-of-anxiety-or-is-it/?_r=0> See also Daniel Smith's *Monkey Mind: A Memoir of Anxiety* (New York: Simon & Schuster, 2012).

[12] "The state of existence is the state of estrangement. Man is estranged from the ground of his being, from other beings, and from himself" (Tillich, *Systematic Theology*, 2:44).

[13] Harvey Cox, "Introduction to the Third Edition," in Tillich, *The Courage to Be*, xvii.

perate longing for connection instead.[14]

It is necessary to point out, however, that while the experience of anxiety in the face of the threat of non-being may be universal, *non-being threatens beings differently.* In other words, to be "shocked" by the possibility of non-being, as Tillich says he was during his military chaplaincy, involves a certain degree of privilege and security. The anxiety and insecurity that are part of being finite[15] will take on a different significance and intensity for those who are viscerally confronted with this threat on a daily basis. Food insecurity is an excellent exemplar in this regard: something shifts in the experience of anxiety—in facing non-being—when the gift of daily bread cannot be relied upon. Tillich's diagnosis of the anxiety that characterizes human life needs to be extended in order to explicitly account for these experiences of members of populations whose potential non-being is ever-present to them. To this end, I want to introduce a concept employed by critical theorist Judith Butler: precarity.

VULNERABLE BODIES

Butler makes a distinction between precariousness and precarity. The fundamental experience all humans have in common is a "shared precariousness."[16] There is a "primary and unwilled physical proximity with others" that characterizes our lives.[17] We are

---

[14] Harvey Cox offers by way of example the frantic dependence on electronic devices that many of us exhibit and diagnoses even this as a quest for connection rather than, as it is most often characterized, a need for distraction. Cox, "Introduction," xvii.

[15] "To be finite is to be insecure" (Tillich, *Systematic Theology*, 1:195).

[16] Judith Butler, *Frames of War: When Is Life Grievable?* (Brooklyn: Verso, 2009) 43.

[17] Judith Butler, *Precarious Life: The Powers of Mourning and Violence* (London: Verso, 2006) 26.

born into relationships we did not choose and are always already dependent upon others not only for our survival but also for our thriving. Each person, each "subject," in Butler's terminology, is best thought of as "a dynamic set of social relations,"[18] relations that render us vulnerable because it is these "primary ties" that either sustain our lives or subject us to violence and violation—we are both made and unmade by these relationships.[19]

Tillich's understanding of the contingency of our lives suggests that he would agree in large part with Butler's articulation of our shared vulnerability. He says, "Contingently we are put into the whole web of causal relations. Contingently we are determined by them in every moment and thrown out by them in the last moment."[20] Butler puts it simply: "Let's face it. We're undone by each other. And if we're not, we're missing something."[21] To an extent, we are all similarly subject to human vulnerability, just as we are all similarly susceptible to the experience of anxiety, rooted in the threat of non-being, that Tillich identifies.

Our bodies are what ensure that we all share this vulnerability; Butler says, "The body implies mortality, vulnerability, agency: the skin and the flesh expose us to the gaze of others, but also to touch, and to violence, and bodies put us at risk of becoming the agency and instrument of all these as well."[22] Our flesh renders each of us vulnerable to others, and it also causes each of us to be *vulnerable to the possibility that we can make others more vulnerable.* Any kind of violence or hostility (or, perhaps, even indifference),

---

[18] Butler, *Frames of War*, 162. Butler sets this up as an alternative to the notion of the autonomous, sovereign individual self that much of the West has absorbed.

[19] Butler, *Precarious Life,* 26–27; see also p. 24.

[20] Tillich, *The Courage to Be,* 42.

[21] Butler, *Precarious Life,* 23.

[22] Ibid., 26.

in Butler's view, results from a lack of recognition that "we are all subject to one another"[23] at the level of our very flesh.

Though all of us live with this fleshy vulnerability, the degree to which it affects each of us varies. To highlight this variance, Butler uses the term "precarity." In Butler's usage, precarity differs from precariousness or vulnerability in that it is unevenly distributed among persons—among bodies—throughout the world. It is a "politically induced condition in which certain populations...become differentially exposed to injury, violence, and death."[24] For Butler, who has been concerned primarily with revealing the mechanisms behind the process of subject formation, the more closely one's behavior and performance approximate the recognizably or acceptably human subject, the less that person's life is affected by precarity. Conversely, the further away one is from embodying the norms of society—the qualities that cause society to count a life as fully, recognizably human—the more one is exposed to precarity. Butler concerned herself initially with what this means for LGBTQ persons who do not conform to the compulsory heterosexuality our culture prescribes,[25] as well as with how this frames the lives of "enemies" the U.S. has fashioned out of religious and political others around the globe in the name of fighting terrorism.[26] Her insights about this "politically induced condition" of precarity provide a useful lens for viewing other kinds of precarious lives beyond these two categories: Butler has

---

[23] Butler, *Frames of War*, 43.

[24] Judith Butler, "Performativity, Precarity, and Sexual Politics," lecture given at Universidad de Complutense de Madrid, 8 June 2009, published in *Revista de Antropología Iberoamericana*, volumen 4, número 3 (Septiembre–Diciembre 2009): i–xiii (ii).

[25] See Judith Butler, *Gender Trouble: Feminism and the Subversion of Identity* (London: Routledge,1989) 190.

[26] See Butler, *Frames of War*, ch. 1.

turned her insights to more recent movements like Occupy Wall Street and Black Lives Matter, identifying those who have been especially vulnerable to abuses of capitalism and to state-sanctioned violence, respectively, as groups experiencing precarity.[27] She leaves plenty of room to identify additional populations along these same lines. One such population, as Butler's attention to the Occupy movement attests, includes the 43.1 million people in the United States whose income places them at or below the poverty line;[28] this population overlaps with the 42.2 million people in the U.S. living in food-insecure households.[29]

It is both unnerving and potentially revolutionary to consider how vulnerable we already are to one another[30]—that is, if we are

---

[27] See her interview with Kyle Bella, "Bodies in Alliance: Gender Theorist Judith Butler on the Occupy and SlutWalk Movements," www.truth-out.org, 15 December 2011 <http://www.truth-out.org/news/item/5588: bodies-in-alliance-gender-theorist-judith-butler-on-the-occupy-and-slutwalk-movements>, and her interview with George Yancy, "What's Wrong with 'All Lives Matter'?" *The New York Times Opinionator Blog*, 12 January 2015 <http://opinionator.blogs.nytimes.com/2015/01/12/whats-wrong-with-all-lives-matter/?_r=0>.

[28] This is according to the most recent census data; the statistic is from 2015 (http://www.census.gov/library/publications/2016/demo/p60-256.html).

[29] Alisha Coleman-Jensen, Matthew P. Rabbitt, Christian A. Gregory, and Anita Singh, "Household Food Security in the United States in 2015," *Economic Research Report* number 215, September 2016 (United States Department of Agriculture Economic Research Service), 6. http://www.ers.usda.gov/webdocs/publications/err215/err-215.pdf.

[30] Theologies of disability—like that of Sharon Betcher—have been crucial in helping make similar observations widely circulated in academic theology. Nancy Eiesland, for example, points out that at some point in life, most people will become either permanently or temporarily disabled, whether by age or disease, so a theology centered on a disabled God is not just for persons who are disabled *now*—we are all vulnerable to physical breakdown. Nancy Eiesland, *The Disabled God: Toward a Liberatory Theology of Disability* (Nashville: Abingdon Press, 1994) 110. See also Courtney Wilder's essay in

not already aware of our own vulnerability on a daily basis. Butler is open to critique on this point. As with Tillich's generalization about people experiencing the shock of non-being, not everyone is likely to experience what we could call Butler's "shock of vulnerability": the most vulnerable among us are aware that they are vulnerable and are reminded of it daily.[31] But Butler's articulation of precarity is intended for those who are not in that position. It is a call to responsibility on the part of those who are less vulnerable to mitigate the vulnerability of those who are more so—not out of a sense of duty or guilt, but because we recognize the vulnerability we share. For Tillich, recognition of our contingency—our non-necessity—is a source of anxiety;[32] yet for Butler, recognition of the vulnerability we share can be fertile soil for solidarity. Giving attention to embodied experience can help account for this difference and illustrates how non-being sometimes produces not only anxiety but also solidarity.

BODILY ANXIETY IN WESTERN CHRISTIANITY

If it is indeed, as Butler suggests, at the site of our skin that we are most vulnerable, it is no wonder that this flesh of ours has

---

this volume that addresses disability theory.

[31] For this reason, the autonomous, independent self that Butler critiques would likely not seem like such a negative thing to a person who had not experienced herself as such. Catherine Keller points to a similar dynamic when she expresses suspicion of the sudden turn to apophaticism—unsaying—in theology just at the time when some are able to speak and be heard. See Catherine Keller, "The Apophasis of Gender: A Fourfold Unsaying of Feminist Theology," *Journal of the American Academy of Religion* 76/4 (December 2008): 911.

[32] Tillich nods to the possibility that the fear of contingency may not be the same in what he calls "collectivistic cultures" as it is in our culture of "individualization," but he nonetheless asserts that collectivistic societies still share a "basic anxiety about death" (Tillich, *The Courage to Be*, 41).

been a source of anxiety in the Christian West for centuries. As is evident by the very existence of this volume, bodies have always been complicated objects of scrutiny for Christian theology. The proliferation of theologies of the body in the past few decades further attests to this fact; theologians who do such work have noted that our embodied selves have been understood as both sites of revelation and experiences of which to be wary—and certain modes of embodiment, of course, have been coded as even less trustworthy than others.[33] We are instructed to deny our flesh, even to crucify it (Gal. 5:24); we are to "put to death" bodily deeds (Rom. 8:13); and our senses are so unreliable they may even cause us to blaspheme (2 Pet. 2:2).

Nonetheless, the Word became flesh and lived in that flesh among us (John 1:1). "Body" became the central metaphor for the church (1 Cor. 12; Rom. 12; Eph. 3–4; Col. 1); the key doctrine that came to set Christianity apart from other traditions was the incarnation of God; and the most widely observed Christian sac-

---

[33] Particularly the bodies of women, who were (and to some extent still are) associated more closely with materiality and "earthiness," and the bodies of non-white people, who have suffered the abuses and indignities of colonialism, slavery, and other forms of state-sanctioned violence in their flesh. Lisa Isherwood and Elizabeth Stuart note this ambivalence and mistrust in their *Introducing Body Theology* (Introductions in Feminist Theology; Sheffield: Sheffield Academic Press, 1998), especially ch. 3, "A Difficult Relationship: Christianity and the Body." Other examples of theologians whose work has drawn attention to this ambivalence include M. Shawn Copeland, *Enfleshing Freedom: Body, Race, and Being* (Minneapolis: Fortress Press, 2009); Karen Teel, *Racism and the Image of God* (New York: Palgrave McMillan, 2010); Marcella Althaus-Reid, *Indecent Theology Theological Perversions in Sex, Gender, and Politics* (London: Routledge, 2000); Jay Emerson Johnson, *Divine Communion: A Eucharistic Theology of Sexual Intimacy* (New York: Seabury Books, 2013); Virginia Burrus, Mark D. Jordan, and Karmen Mackendrick, *Seducing Augustine: Bodies, Desires, Confessions* (New York: Fordham University Press, 2010).

rament involves eating the body of this enfleshed God, symbolically or otherwise. And the apparent disavowals of embodiment serve
only to highlight its power: though often ambivalent, musings on
flesh and the body saturate the scriptures, serving to underscore
materiality's importance, not unravel it.[34] These bodies we inhabit
are sources of both deep pleasure and deep pain—both joy and,
yes, anxiety.[35]

Of all the bodily processes that have preoccupied and per-
plexed us, sex and eating seem to have caused the most consterna-
tion. Scholars speculate that this is because sex and eating are "activities that reveal most potently the permeability of bodily
boundaries."[36] These two activities bring our fleshy vulnerability

---

[34] A distinction between the notion of "body" and the notion of "flesh"
is helpful here, but an extended treatment of this distinction lies beyond the
scope of this chapter. For articulations of the ways flesh (*sarx*) and body (*so-
ma*) would have been related in the minds of early Christians and the ways
their usage has shifted over time, see Dale B. Martin, *The Corinthian Body*
(New Haven: Yale University Press, 1995), as well as the essays in Clare K.
Rothschild and Trevor W. Thompson, eds., *Christian Body, Christian Self:
Concepts of Early Christian Personhood* (Tübingen: Mohr Siebeck, 2011).

[35] Devan Stahl graciously and helpfully pointed out the problems that
come with claiming that we *are* bodies rather than that we *have* bodies. For
those whose bodies feel alien or hostile—those living with chronic illness or
disability, those whose gender identities do not match their birth-assigned
sex, etc.—being completely identified with one's body can be stifling. Her
essay engaging transhumanism in this volume touches on these issues as well
(ch. 7).

"Inhabit" is the best way I can think of to express how we relate to our
bodies that leans into the tension between being bodies and having bodies.
My intention is to follow Nancy Eiesland's insight that each of us experiences embodiment in its "jumbled pleasure-pain," but perhaps none more so
than people with disabilities. See Eiesland, *The Disabled God*, 96.

[36] David Grumett, "Dynamics of Christian Dietary Abstinence," in *Religion, Food, and Eating in North America*, ed. Benjamin E. Zeller, Marie W.
Dallam, Reid L. Neilson, and Nora L. Rubel (New York: Columbia University Press, 2014) 3–22 (5). Anthropologist Mary Douglas brought much of

into sharpest relief—for both, we are dependent on something outside of ourselves, and both play a role in our survival either as individuals or as a species. Eating and sex were united from the very beginning of the Judeo-Christian narrative in the eyes of many of the early church theologians—some interpretations of Genesis 3 suggest "that gluttony was the cardinal sin, which engendered all others,"[37] leading to the association of "immoderate eating" with sexual licentiousness.[38]

For the early church, food was also a preoccupation because of how eating and faithfulness were variously connected in light of the dietary practices prescribed by the Torah. We can see this concern in the story of Peter's encounter with the Gentile Cornelius in Acts 10, when Peter must come to terms with the fact that eating in obedience to God might look a bit different now: in the way Paul must engage the Corinthian church's confusion over what to do about food sacrificed to idols (1 Cor. 8), and in the way early Christians absorbed the Greek emphasis on maintaining control over natural bodily appetites in order to be properly attuned to spiritual development.[39] Later, some desert fathers and mothers even contemplated food's moral status, concluding that food was not necessary prior to the fall, and therefore not just eating but *all* "the functions that food sustained were necessarily sinful."[40]

Consideration of the relationship between food and spiritual

---

this to light in her work, most notably *Purity and Danger: An Analysis of Concepts of Pollution and Taboo* (London and New York: Routledge, 1966), in which she illuminated the way permeation of bodily boundaries is at the root of many of the taboos that came to be codified into ancient law, like the Levitical purity laws and holiness codes.

[37] Grumett, "Dynamics," 7.

[38] Ibid., 5.

[39] See John Coveney, *Food, Morals, and Meaning: The Pleasure and Anxiety of Eating*, 2nd ed. (London and New York: Routledge, 2006) 9 and ch. 3.

[40] Grumett, "Dynamics," 15.

development in later eras focused on various understandings of fasting. For early modern Protestants, seeking to remove themselves from the strictures of Roman Catholic rituals, ascetic practices like fasting needed to be rethought, but they were still held in high regard. It was generally believed that fasting and experiencing induced hunger were signifiers of holiness: "Fasting raised prayer to higher levels of zeal and also of power, according to believers: God would more readily answer prayers that were accompanied by sincere and rigorous abstinence. Hunger was also intended to remind individuals of their fragile humanity and dependence on God..."[41] If one was too sated, too comfortable, one ran the risk of being distanced from God—yet fasting too fastidiously tempted the faster to become prideful in his or her piety.

Though never definitive, concern about food through Christian history highlights how important it has been and continues to be. Table fellowship was a staple of the early church, and the echoes of this have reverberated throughout modern Western Christian history, from Wesleyan "love feasts" in the eighteenth century to ubiquitous church potlucks in the twentieth. Eating together is a way to express love and commitment to the community of faith, even though food and our natural appetites are still thought to pose a threat in some ways.

Today, general anxieties over food take a slightly different shape, yet they still carry echoes of these earlier worries. The early modern Protestant association of holiness with being in control of one's body (which itself echoes patristic and medieval constructs) contributed to the diet and fitness culture that has saturated twentieth- and twenty-first-century Protestantism in the U.S.; some expressions of this culture have promoted unrealistic, unhealthy,

---

[41] Marie Griffith, *Born-Again Bodies* (Berkeley and Los Angeles: University of California Press, 2004) 31.

and often racist, classist, and able-ist constructions of the ideal body.[42] Partly because of this history, varying relationships with our own embodiment may cause us to look at food as a threat. For those who experience disordered eating, for example, food may be either an enemy to be avoided or a hollow comfort used to temporarily quiet emotional turmoil. Anxiety may also arise when we are confronted with the multiple ethical issues that arise in considering the sourcing of our food, particularly in the face of globalization; it is difficult to consistently purchase groceries that are locally sourced, ethically grown and raised, *and* affordable. Wellness culture adds another layer to this stress—what is the best diet to adopt in order to mitigate harm to both one's body and the planet?[43]

HUNGER, FOOD INSECURITY, AND ESTRANGEMENT

---

[42] See Griffith, *Born-Again Bodies,* who observes, "The body, whatever else it is, is the fundamental matter upon which diverse politics of exclusion operate" (10); see also ch. 5. See also Lisa Isherwood, *The Fat Jesus: Christianity and Body Image* (Harrisburg: Seabury Books, 2008) 2: "…size carries with it a gendered rhetoric about moral goodness and sanctity."

[43] To this point, a noticeable shift has taken place in the publishing industry from cookbooks featuring foods that are comforting, hearty, and delicious to those that focus on "wellness" and tend to engender guilt and anxiety over not eating the "right" way. See Ruby Tandoh's recent investigation of this phenomenon and its effects: "The Unhealthy Truth Behind 'Wellness' and 'Clean Eating,'" *Vice,* May 13, 2016 < http://www.vice.com/en_uk/read/ruby-tandoh-eat-clean-wellness>. It is worth noting, however, that even this recent development has a lineage that can be traced to early modern Protestantism: Mary Mann, the wife of educational reformer Horace Mann, wrote and published *Christianity in the Kitchen: A Physiological Cookbook,* which advised simple, clean eating to keep the digestive tract in good working order *as part of holy living,* in 1858. The full text of the cookbook is available here: https://archive.org/details/christianityinki00mann. See also Daniel Sack, *Whitebread Protestants: Food and Religion in American Culture* (Basingstoke: Palgrave Macmillan, 2000) 191–93.

Perhaps no experience of food-related anxiety matches the specific mode of existential anxiety that Tillich names better than the experience of those for whom food is scarce, of low quality, and lacking in nutritional value. To live with food insecurity is to live with both the condition of precarity that Butler identifies and an acute sense of the anxiety that Tillich names.

Few things remind us of our finitude quite like the physical experience of hunger. Norman Wirzba puts the tension well when he writes, "Though eating can be among our most pleasurable acts, it is also inherently troubling because we know that we will have to eat again."[44] Satisfying a bodily need reminds us of our potential non-being—we are dependent on the repeated satisfaction of our hunger in order to survive. Fasting, as noted above, taps into this sensibility by marking our dependence on God by limiting consumption. This daily reminder of finitude is more present, however, for those who are not hungry *by choice*. While all of us require nutrition to live and are therefore *vulnerable*, not all of us experience the *precarity* of food insecurity.

As noted above, food insecurity affects roughly 42.2 million people in the United States: about one in every eight people live in households that experience food insecurity. The condition of food insecurity (which includes but is not limited to the condition of hunger) occurs when a person or family lacks reliable and consistent "physical and economic access to sufficient, safe, and nutritious food that meets their dietary needs and food preferences for an active and healthy life."[45] The World Health Organization has

---

[44] Norman Wirzba, *Food and Faith: A Theology of Eating* (New York: Cambridge University Press, 2011) 29.

[45] As defined at the 1996 World Food Summit, cited in the FAO Food Security Information for Action guide, "An Introduction to the Basic Concepts of Food Security," http://www.fao.org/docrep/013/al936e/al936-e00.pdf.

a more expansive definition and includes the caveats that, in order to be food-secure, a person must have access to food that is culturally acceptable; and the means by which the food was produced must be ecologically sustainable, ethical, and "obtained in a manner that upholds human dignity."[46]

For people who live in urban or rural food deserts, for example, where a personal vehicle or reliable and affordable public transportation is hard to come by, *physical* access to good food is diminished.[47] For people whose nearest grocery store is a Whole Foods or other specialty retailer, *economic* access to food may be diminished. The selection of food products available in corner convenience stores, perhaps the closest thing to a grocery store within easy walking distance in some neighborhoods, is limited (customers may not be able to choose according to their food *preferences*) and may include products that are well past their expiration dates (this food is not *safe*) and are prepackaged rather than fresh (typically not *nutritious*). Recently-arrived immigrants may not be able to find food that is *culturally acceptable*; much of our

---

[46] Nutrition and Food Security Programme, "First Action Plan for Food and Nutrition Policy" (World Health Organization Regional Committee for Europe, 2001) 32–33. Devan Stahl pointed out that this broader definition could indicate that almost *all* of us are food-insecure—little of the food making its way through the U.S. food system is sourced in the ethical and sustainable way that this definition prescribes, for example. Analysis of this point lies beyond the scope of this chapter.

[47] The term "food desert" has come under some critical scrutiny recently. It may not be the most apt way to describe what is at the root of the U.S.'s hunger problem (but is still a widely used term in the field). Studies within the past few years have shown that it is not simply proximity to stores that affects food insecurity; economic inequality is the larger issue that must be addressed. For perspective on this, see Joe Cortright, "Are Food Deserts to Blame for America's Poor Eating Habits?" *The Atlantic*, 9 November 2015. https://www.theatlantic.com/business/archive/2015/11/food-deserts/41453-4/.

food is neither grown nor sourced *ethically*; and if a family must submit to drug screening before obtaining SNAP benefits, their food is not being acquired in a way that promotes their *dignity*.[48]

Far from a wider concern for dignity, early government efforts to address hunger in the United States were practical and emerged in response to the Great Depression. The federal government began to purchase agricultural surplus from farmers who could not sell all that they produced and used the surplus to feed hungry families through the work of the Red Cross.[49] The 1960s brought the development of the food-stamp program and WIC (Women, Infants, and Children). Hunger spiked in the 1980s due to a recession, but the Reagan administration's policies on the food-stamp program limited the ways people could access groceries for their families.[50]

Because of the federal government's cuts to assistance programs, the responsibility of addressing food insecurity fell to private organizations, such as faith-based community food banks. These kinds of organizations grew drastically in the 1980s to meet the growing needs of more and more people who could not otherwise get sufficient supplemental nutrition.[51] Hunger seems to be one effect of poverty that Americans are unwilling to overlook. "Whether as a result of fundamental religious teachings or innate

---

[48] The 2015 Wisconsin state budget bill mandated that applicants for SNAP benefits submit to drug screening. Other states have included such regulations for those who apply for many different federal assistance programs.

[49] "Hunger and Food Security," *Food System Primer,* Johns Hopkins Center for a Livable Future < http://www.foodsystemprimer.org/food-and-nutrition/hunger-and-food-insecurity/>.

[50] Sack, *Whitebread Protestants,* 108; see also Mark Winne, *Closing the Food Gap: Resetting the Table in the Land of Plenty* (Boston: Beacon Press, 2008) ch. 2.

[51] "Hunger and Food Insecurity."

human compassion, most of us will do what we can to prevent a fellow human being from teetering too close to the brink of starvation."[52] Daniel Sack even suggests that feeding hungry people has taken the place of traditional evangelism in liberal mainline Protestant communities in the U.S.[53] Yet, these efforts on the part of both the government and church-based organizations have mostly been in the form of emergency food assistance—and this assistance has not been without its critics.

As far back as the 1930s, when the federal government first intervened noticeably in the problem of hunger in the U.S., critics voiced concerns about the potential threat to the national work ethic as well as the threat to basic human dignity that "handouts" posed.[54] Other critiques since that time have included observations that participating in emergency food aid gives the illusion of contributing to a solution to hunger, but in reality such efforts mostly provide a salve for the conscience of the privileged person who cannot or will not acknowledge the more difficult, systemic issues that perpetuate the precarity of food-insecure people. Emergency food aid deals with the symptoms rather than the problem itself, but participating in hunger relief in this way makes people feel as though they are contributing to solving a problem. A critic of emergency food aid in the 1970s put it more bluntly: "'apolitical' charity is more popular with American supporters, who know that supporting social change could erode their own privileged posi-

---

[52] Winne, *Closing the Food Gap,* xx.

[53] Sack, *Whitebread Protestants,* 133.

[54] "Hunger and Food Insecurity"; see also Dennis Roth, *Food Stamps: 1932–1977: From Provisional and Pilot Programs to Permanent Policy,* U.S. Department of Agriculture Rural Information Center, (archived) <https://pubs.nal.usda.gov/sites/pubs.nal.usda.gov/files/foodstamps.html> (cited in "Hunger and Food Insecurity").

tion."[55]

These systemic problems cannot be ignored. The disparity between people living with food insecurity and those who do not experience this form of precarity has not decreased since it was first noted in the 1960s and 1970s. Known as the "food gap," this disparity has largely remained constant over the decades since it was identified, and it has even increased in recent years. One reason for the widening food gap is that when those living with food insecurity or insufficiency finally achieve a base level of access to food, groups in higher economic brackets drive the market for some new health trend or expensive organic (or industrial-organic) foods. Mark Winne puts it this way: "In other words, as trends in consumption associated with lifestyle and health expand one class's universe of choice and perceived health benefits, a lower, less privileged class barely catches up to where the other class was in the last decade."[56]

Food and our eating habits are intimately connected to these wider social issues. The growth of the academic field of foodways studies demonstrates that food carries with it social, emotional, spiritual/religious, political, and economic meaning; it is not merely a source of fuel. Martha Finch notes, "...not only does [food] provide physical nourishment and sustenance, but those who eat also invest what is (and is not) eaten with deep and compelling values. That is, food serves as both material element and sacred symbol...food nourishes both body and soul."[57] The link between

---

[55] Sack, *Whitebread Protestants*, 162.

[56] Winne, *Closing the Food Gap*, xix.

[57] Martha L. Finch, "Foreword," in *Religion, Food, and Eating in North America*, ed. Benjamin E. Zeller, Marie W. Dallam, Reid L. Neilson, and Nora L. Rubel (New York: Columbia University Press, 2014) xi. Of course, the converse is also true: food has been thought to impact both body and soul negatively as well and has therefore been a source of fracturing and fragmen-

physical and spiritual nourishment is strong, and it points to why food has been at the center of so much spiritual and communal life in the church. Food insecurity can be a source of the kind of existential anxiety that Tillich identifies precisely because it is so much more than a merely material concern.[58] Yet, the very material reality of food and eating—that we must always eat again—is what heightens the sense of existential anxiety that food insecurity can produce. Living with uncertainty about where one's next meal is coming from or whether it will be sufficiently nutritious to ensure good health harms both bodies and minds. Food insecurity and insufficiency are linked not only to malnutrition and other physical ailments but also to anxiety, depression, and other mental-health issues in children who live in food-insecure households, and these issues are compounded by the anxiety that their caregivers experience and pass along to children through emotional cues.[59]

---

tation. See, for example, in *Born-Again Bodies,* where Griffith details how diet culture today implicitly promotes the belief that "[t]he body is a hazard to the soul, able to demolish the hardest won spiritual gains merely through ingesting the wrong material" (2), and, "Fit bodies ostensibly signify fitter souls" (6). See also Daniel Sack, *Whitebread Protestants,* who observes, "Food carries moral value in America. In this culture, a particular foodstuff is not only good or bad for your body but also can be good or bad for your soul," and he gives the example of desserts being called "sinful" (186). Sack also offers a deep-dive into several instances in which the connection between eating habits and spiritual health affected Christian practice and teaching. For example, some Christians early in the temperance movement joined the fight because they believed that imbibing alcohol carried with it the threat of being "damned as well as diseased" (14).

[58] See Tillich, *The Courage to Be,* 42–43.

[59] Maureen Black, "Household Food Insecurities: Threats to Children's Well-Being," *The SES Indicator,* June 2012, American Psychological Association <https://www.apa.org/pi/ses/resources/indicator/2012/06/household-food-insecurities.aspx>. See a summary of similar findings in "Child Food Insecurity and Mental Health," McSilver Institute for Poverty Policy and Research, New York University http://mcsilver.nyu.edu/sites/default/files/

As previously indicated, the existential anxiety Tillich describes is related to estrangement—estrangement both from the ground of being and from one another. This estrangement appears when we forget our connections with one another and treat one another as objects. He contends that prevailing or "controlling knowledge" has resulted in "a rapid decay of spiritual...life, an estrangement from nature, and, most dangerous of all, a dealing with human beings as with things."[60] For Tillich, the "[t]reasures of empirical knowledge" so prized in the modern era have edged out and taken precedence over "[t]hat which can be known only by participation and union," that is, our fellow humans and the divine.[61]

We could think of the political ramifications of the food gap as one symptom of the estrangement that Tillich names. Food-insecure people become statistics—a problem to be solved—rather than human beings with complex lives, desires, and a need for connection. No wonder emergency food aid has not been able to shrink the gap. A broader, more holistic response is needed, one that takes into account the various ways that systems of power have damaged our "primary ties" (to use Butler's words) and ad-

---

Child%20Food%20Insecurity%20and%20Mental%20Health.pdf. Similarly, research published by the Academic Pediatric Association shows that "[a]dolescents living in households with food insecurity are at increased risk for parent-reported mental-health problems, even after adjusting for other risk factors," and while providing these adolescents with programs such as free or reduced school lunches may address the hunger question, mental-health intervention is also necessary. Elizabeth Pool-Di Salvo, Ellen J. Silver, and Ruth E.K. Stein, "Household Food Insecurity and Mental-Health Problems Among Adolescents: What Do Parents Report?" *Academic Pediatrics* 16/1 (2016): 90–96 (90). http://www.sciencedirect.com/science/article/pii/S1876285915002727.

[60] Tillich, *Systematic Theology*, 1:99.
[61] Ibid.

dresses the anxiety of living in this state of precarity.

Other symptoms of a Tillichian estrangement are evident, socially, in the way our food culture has developed. Wirzba calls the phenomenon "eating in exile" and says, "[W]hen we eat in exile we eat alone and with considerable violence, without deep connection or affection, experiencing food and each other as mere objects and threats or as the means to our power, control, and convenience."[62] The way we eat, especially in the United States, in other words—largely cut off both from the earthy processes and places that produce our food and from the people who are involved in the beginning stages of its transformation into what we eventually eat; isolated in our cars as we scarf down drive-through meals on our way to the next thing crowding our lives; etc.—is further evidence of our estrangement.[63]

---

[62] Wirzba, *Food and Faith*, 77.

[63] The "slow-food movement," made famous by Berkeley-based chef Alice Waters of the restaurant Chez Panisse, as well as the work of journalist Michael Pollan (most notably in his book *The Omnivore's Dilemma: A Natural History of Four Meals* [New York: The Penguin Press, 2006]), have gone a long way toward making Americans in some circles newly aware of where our food comes from. Two additional examples may serve to begin to illustrate the phenomenon of estrangement and eating in exile. One is the way American Indian/First Nations people have been divorced from the land since the westward expansion of Euro-American settlers. For example, on the Pine Ridge reservation in South Dakota, many residents—Lakota Sioux people whose primary connection to the land, Grandmother Earth, was integral to their identity and that of their ancestors—now wait in lines at the Sioux Nation Shopping Center (the main grocery store on the reservation) for the clock to strike midnight on the tenth of every month when their EBT (electronic benefit transfer) cards automatically recharge, so they can spend their government benefits on processed and packaged foods. Due to multiple systemic injustices that have accumulated over generations, they have been cut off from the ability to access culturally meaningful foods on a regular basis. For a glimpse into the multiple issues of food safety, accessibility, and poverty that this market reveals, see Daniel Simmons-Ritchie, "Anger at tribe's

Finally, we are exiled not only from one another, but also from our own bodily life. This distance from "biological reality" hinders our ability to acknowledge our dependence on and vulnerability to the other creatures with whom we share the earth. Wendell Berry puts it perhaps most damningly when he writes,

> The passive American consumer, sitting down to a meal of pre-prepared or fast food, confronts a platter covered with inert, anonymous substances that have been processed, dyed, breaded, sauced, gravied, ground, pulped, strained, blended, prettified, and sanitized beyond resemblance to any part of any creature that ever lived....Both eater and eaten are thus in exile from biological reality.[64]

LOVE, COURAGE, AND JUSTICE:

ALTERNATIVE RESPONSES TO HUNGER

How do we begin to craft a theological answer to the question that arises from anxieties over food? For Tillich, we begin with love. When Tillich states, "Love has been more and more acknowledged as the answer to the question implied in anxiety and neurosis,"[65] he is not only naming a trend but also affirming a

---

decision to close Pine Ridge's sole supermarket," *Rapid City Journal,* online edition, 26 May 2013 <http://rapidcityjournal.com/news/anger-at-tribe-s-decision-to-close-pine-ridge-s/article_1032f0f3-0bf1-5296-9b6b-64a46f447e1b.html>. The supermarket remains open. Another example is simply the process of producing industrial bread: Expensive machines and devices—combines, grain elevators, factory mills—control the process from beginning to end. These days, "[h]uman hands never touch the grain, flour, or dough" (Winne, *Closing the Food Gap,* 7).

[64] Wendell Berry, "The Pleasures of Eating," in *What Are People For?* (Berkeley: Counterpoint, 2010), excerpted in Sandra M. Gilbert and Roger J. Porter, eds., *Eating Words: A Norton Anthology of Food Writing* (New York and London: W.W. Norton & Company, 2015) 381–85.

[65] Paul Tillich, *Love, Power, and Justice* (Oxford; New York: Oxford

truth.

Love is the vehicle for the reconciliation that overcomes estrangement. It sounds too simple—until we discover precisely what Tillich means by "love." Tillich acknowledges the goodness of the forms of love known as *libido, philia,* and *erōs* in our human interactions but says the highest form of love is *agapē,* in which we go beyond desiring our own fulfillment and instead desire that the other be fulfilled (or, perhaps for our purposes, *filled*).[66] This kind of love "affirms the other unconditionally" and is associated with morality and justice for Tillich.[67] Moreover, to behave morally is "to become what one potentially is, a *person* within a community of persons."[68] For Tillich, "The destiny of the individual cannot be separated from the destiny of the whole in which it participates."[69] We are contingent creatures, after all, as Tillich reminds us.

This means there is no flourishing for me unless there is flourishing for my neighbor, our community, and the earth that gives life to us all. Tillich is here speaking back to the same addiction to the illusion of individualism that Butler critiques; it seems he would acknowledge what she describes as "the thrall in which

---

University Press, 1954) 22–23.

[66] As Adam Pryor has helpfully pointed out, Tillich's emphasis on *agapē* is open to critique; his insistence on the role of desire in this kind of love indicates that *erōs* in fact plays a larger role than he seems willing to admit. See, for instance, Adam Pryor, *Body of Christ Incarnate for You: Conceptualizing God's Desire for the Flesh,* Studies in Body and Religion (Lanham: Lexington, 2016) ch. 3; and Jan-Olav Henriksen, "Eros and/as Desire—A Theological Affirmation: Paul Tillich Read in the Light of Jean-Luc Marion's The Erotic Phenomenon," *Modern Theology* 26/2 (April 2010): 220–42.

[67] Tillich, *Systematic Theology,* 1:281. Tillich prefers the term "morality" to "ethics" when discussing the action of love. On this point see Paul Tillich, *Morality & Beyond,* rev. ed., Library of Theological Ethics (Louisville: Westminster John Knox Press, 1995 [1963]) 22.

[68] Tillich, *Morality & Beyond,* 19.

[69] Tillich, *Systematic Theology,* 1:270.

our relations with others hold us."[70] The recognition of this inter-dependence—*this vulnerability to the destinies of vulnerable others*—may be part of what Tillich has in mind when he asserts, "[E]very moral act includes a risk. The human situation itself is such a risk,"[71] and, moreover, "Love is creative and creativity includes risk."[72] Tillich seems to have in mind certain aspects of the risk of connection with others—a participation for which we all long, but which requires vulnerability. And, as we have seen, the human situation is riskier for some than for others—this is what precarity helps us to identify.

Contemporary theologians like Catherine Keller may help us extend Tillich's vision of this risky love beyond what he may have been able to imagine. Keller would have us amend Tillich's asser-tion that love is the answer to a question; rather, love *is* the ques-tion—or is at least worth calling into question.[73] We cannot do without it, but we must resist the impulse to "overname" what is meant by it. Thus, Keller proposes retrieving the apophatic way that the Apostle Paul expresses love: a way present even in his most famous declaration of what love *is,* 1 Corinthians 13. Mela-nie Johnson-DeBaufre points out that most of the definition here comes from articulations of what love is *not*—as she says, "Love exposes not-love,"[74] and this leaves us some room to imagine what love could possibly look like in every new context.

---

[70] Butler, *Precarious Life,* 23.

[71] Paul Tillich, *Theology of Culture* (New York: Oxford University Press, 1978 [1959]) 140.

[72] Tillich, *Theology of Culture,* 145.

[73] "What a questionable notion. Love, just as wastefully overnamed as its most solemn metonym, God" (Catherine Keller, *Cloud of the Impossible: Negative Theology and Planetary Entanglement* [New York: Columbia Univer-sity Press, 2014] 288).

[74] Quoted in ibid., 300.

We might add another example of this "not-love" from Romans, where we started above: "If your brother or sister is being injured by what you eat, you are no longer walking in love" (14:15a, NRSV). This is what not-love looks like: the injury of a brother or sister because of selfish or thoughtless eating choices. The Greek-translated "injured" here in the NRSV is from *lupeō*: "to cause severe mental or emotional distress, vex, irritate, offend, insult"; to "be distressed"; or to "grieve."[75] With regard to its use in this particular passage, the BDAG offers, "*if a member's feelings are hurt because of food*," then notes parenthetically, "but [lupeō] can also mean *injure, damage*."[76] With some linguistic liberties, I might go so far as to interpret it as "to wound": in the Latin, *vulnerare*. To make vulnerable. Perhaps Paul's words mean this for us today: if my brother or sister is made more vulnerable, weaker, more precarious—more readily confronted by his or her own non-being—by what and how I choose to eat, this is not-love. By recognizing the ways food always already connects us and renders us vulnerable—and viewing that vulnerability not as a liability but as a gift[77]—we can perhaps begin instead to "walk in love" in this way with both our local and our global neighbors.

With the savvy lawyer in Luke 10, we may be tempted to ask, "And who is my neighbor?" Tillich answers: My neighbor is anyone "with whom a concrete relation is technically possible."[78] Even the neighbors I don't know yet. I may not know what it looks like to love them, but I know what it looks like to not-love them.

Today, this community—the pool of others "with whom a

---

[75] Frederick William Danker, *A Greek-English Lexicon of the New Testament and Other Early Christian Literature* (BDAG), 3rd ed., s.v. "λυπέω" (Chicago: University of Chicago Press, 2000).

[76] Danker, *A Greek-English Lexicon*.

[77] Again, vulnerability is not a gift when it results in oppression.

[78] Tillich, *Systematic Theology*, 1:270.

concrete relation is technically possible"—is a global one, and learning how to love our brothers and sisters is not often simple or pure. In fact, more often than not, "even where [love] works, it tangles."[79] Keller wisely observes that "life together does not get more convivial as it gets planetary."[80] As our connections multiply, so does the potential for harm even when we are trying to act in love.[81] For example, in the 1960s and 1970s, as the U.S. began to turn its attention to alleviating hunger abroad, the efficient and effective farming techniques and technologies we exported were simultaneously mitigating hunger *and* creating a dependence on foreign oil, embedding then-developing nations in power structures that were detrimental to their growth and making famine even worse during the energy crisis of the 1970s.[82] According to Keller, as we follow the biblical witness that promotes an apophatic understanding of love, we are always just feeling our way toward what love looks like in a given situation, and sometimes the best we can do is avoid the not-love. Perhaps love rooted in the courage of facing our vulnerability simply strives to lean meaningfully into the relationships and power structures that have become warped and unsustainable.

---

[79] Keller, *Cloud of the Impossible*, 302.

[80] Keller, *Cloud of the Impossible*, 302.

[81] Even this chapter likely perpetuates some undesirable stereotypes and assumptions, even while in it I try to make some advance against such things.

[82] Sack, *Whitebread Protestants*, 161–62.

EATING OUR WAY TOWARD SOLIDARITY

One place I am trying to work out what this love looks like is in the classroom. I live and teach in Nashville, Tennessee, one of the fastest-growing cities in the United States.[83] I teach a first-year seminar titled "You Are What You Eat: Food, Faith, Ethics, and Identity." One of the explicit aims for this course is to help students understand themselves as "citizens of multiple communities," to get to know their new home and figure out how to become woven into the fabric of the community—perhaps, per Tillich, more consciously to become "*person*[s] within a community of persons."[84] Nashville is a perfect place to use food to access that consciousness, because part of the appeal that is bringing new residents to Nashville is the emerging food scene. New restaurants by nationally and internationally renowned chefs are opening all the time. Residents frequent food trucks that specialize in reinventions of traditional Southern cuisine. The "slow-food" movement, whose U.S. incarnation is commonly associated with the San Francisco Bay area, has made its way to the South, and we are seeing the rise of restaurants that feature seasonal, local, and sustainable cuisine (or at least claim to do so). Nashville is, in other words, becoming a haven for foodies, as are many other cities around the U.S. At the same time, food insecurity is rampant; indeed, "of the counties in the top 10 percent of food insecurity, 90 percent of them are located in the South."[85] Davidson County, where Nashville is situated, has a food-insecurity rate of 17.4 percent, when

---

[83] At the time of writing, it was the 25th-largest city in the nation, with around 660,000 people.

[84] Tillich, *Morality & Beyond,* 19.

[85] Josh Rosenblat, "America doesn't have a food problem. It has a hunger problem," vox.com, 29 April 2016, http://www.vox.com/2016/4/29/11521610/hunger-food-insecurity-food-stamps.

last measured (compared to the national average of 14%). In one recent year, the number of pounds of food distributed via emergency food aid in Nashville increased by 11 percent. Because of the rapid growth of the city and the rising cost of living, the number of requests for emergency food assistance continues to increase substantially, even while the resources available to provide that assistance decrease. New high-end housing developments downtown mean that longtime residents are being pushed out of central locations and into so-called food deserts. (Also, those seasonal, local, and sustainable meals at the slow-food restaurants are provided at a price point out of reach for most people to enjoy on a regular basis.) This is not an unfamiliar paradox for many of us in the cities where we live.[86] Sharon Betcher is right that something about urban life enables citizens "to avoid carrying the burden of the other" and to become "invulnerable to interdependence"[87]—or at least to imagine ourselves to be so. In my course, I want to help students (and myself) avoid these temptations. One of the ways I try to do this—and try to help these students get to know their new home—is by having them participate in service learning with partner agencies in Nashville that seek to address the food gap in our city.

Some students spend time preparing and serving lunch at a

---

[86] Of course, urban areas are not the only or even the primary places where food insecurity is prevalent; rural areas are some of the most affected. There is often unconscious bias regarding race and geography that seeps into analyses of who counts as food-insecure. For example, people who live in rural areas "are considered by the USDA to have adequate food access if they live within 10 miles of a grocery store, whereas otherwise identical urban residents are considered to have adequate access only if they live within a mile or half-mile of a store" (Cortright, "Are Food Deserts to Blame for America's Poor Eating Habits?").

[87] Sharon V. Betcher, *Spirit and the Obligation of Social Flesh: A Secular Theology for the Global City* (New York: Fordham University Press, 2014) 33.

local soup kitchen. Other students have engaged in SNAP advocacy work, helping eligible citizens navigate the application process for federal assistance. Another group worked in urban gardens with an agency that uses the garden as an educational tool with local public-school students as well as community members. Others spend their time at a local food bank, sorting products that have been donated or obtained through "grocery-rescue" programs (in which the food bank receives surplus products that would have been discarded by local grocery stores, either due to slightly damaged packaging, looming expiration dates, or misshapen produce that typical customers do not choose).[88]

My students learn a great deal through this work; they gain a new perspective and come away from these experiences feeling deeply grateful for their own food security. But they are mostly involved in forms of emergency food aid and are not always asked by these agencies to confront larger systemic issues or to recognize their own vulnerability and thus acknowledge how close they could be to the precarity of the people they are serving. The power dynamic between the person serving and the person being served is maintained. This work by itself does not create space for students to run the risk of "erod[ing] their own privileged position"[89] and acknowledge the ways that even their efforts at helping may in some ways harm. That risk—the one of allowing the precarity of our neighbors to make plain our own precariousness—must be taken in the process of reflecting together on these experiences, and of making the effort to listen to the stories of these neighbors and taking them as seriously as our own stories.

---

[88] The agencies with which we have partnered for this class are Second Harvest Food Bank of Middle Tennessee, Community Food Advocates, Luke 14:12, The Nashville Food Project, and Hands On Nashville.

[89] Sack, *Whitebread Protestants*, 169.

Perhaps Wendell Berry puts the whole complicated mess perfectly when he says,

> It is possible—as our experience in this good land shows—to exile ourselves from Creation, and to ally ourselves with the principle of destruction—which is, ultimately, the principle of nonentity. It is to be willing in general for beings to not-be....That is not to suggest that we can live harmlessly, or strictly at our own expense; we depend upon other creatures and survive by their deaths. To live, we must daily break the body and shed the blood of Creation. When we do this knowingly, lovingly, skillfully, reverently, it is a sacrament. When we do it ignorantly, greedily, clumsily, destructively, it is a desecration. In such desecration we condemn ourselves to spiritual and moral loneliness, and others to want.[90]

An instance of not-love occurs each time we to choose to eat in exile, "ignorantly, greedily, clumsily, destructively," as Berry puts it. Addressing the existential anxiety caused by food insecurity cannot take place only through emergency food aid. The problem is deeper than that. It is a fundamental estrangement from the entire process that enables food to connect us to one another and to the rest of creation (and, by extension, to the creator, the ground of being). The recognition that we are all vulnerable to being cut off from these processes—and in many ways already are, as Wirzba has observed in naming our "eating in exile"—has the potential to help overcome that estrangement.

Now, perhaps more than ever (or at least now more than many of us can remember), we need people who will lean into anxiety in the name of love, demonstrating genuine courage in the face of the threat of annihilation. One small way to do this would

---

[90] Wendell Berry, "The Gift of Good Land," in *The Gift of Good Land: Further Essays Cultural and Agricultural* (Berkeley: Counterpoint, 2009) 281.

be to eat our way toward solidarity, and teach our students and those in our other circles of accountability to do the same. We all eat. We may as well do it together.

4

"Tell Me I Ain't God's Son": Reading Tupac's Stigmatized Body as a Religious Symbol

TYLER ATKINSON

Two years ago, I began teaching an interdisciplinary course called, "Jesus Walks: Explorations into African-American Music and Religion." As a white guy teaching in the Midwest post-Ferguson, I wanted to perform a kind of midwifery service, sharing the wisdom of Black religion in America—expressed by the likes of Blind Willie Johnson, Mahalia Jackson, and Common on the one hand, and James Hal Cone, Eboni Marshall Turman, and Willie James Jennings on the other—with a diverse group of students, most of whom had likely signed up for the course because they could "get their religion credits out of the way" by listening to a lot of music. That semester, we supplemented our daily listening assignments from the course's Spotify playlist with ritualistic readings from Ta-Nehisi Coates's *Between the World and Me* at the beginning of each class session. Though I had not framed the course in Tillichian terms, the Black body was its ultimate concern, a concern that made students who looked like me uncomfortable (perhaps as all witnesses of the grotesquerie of the cross are made to feel) but which, on its best days, at the very least challenged students to rethink the subjects of their own concern as well as the symbols they cherished.

That first iteration of the course followed Black music and religion in America relatively chronologically, which meant that we ended the course with a focus on hip hop,[1] particularly Kendrick Lamar's *To Pimp a Butterfly*, which would go on to win the 2015 GRAMMY award for Best Rap Album.[2] This section of the course was energizing. It was not simply that hip hop was a "relevant" cultural form that met the students "where they were." Rather, in the aftermath of Ferguson and Baltimore, hip hop music from the likes of Kendrick Lamar was as politically relevant as it was aesthetically pleasing. Even as his music made students "bounce to the beat," Lamar was explicitly drawing attention to the harsh realities surrounding mass incarceration. Yet, in doing so, he was simply drawing on a rich tradition already present in hip hop music.

Therefore, the next version of the course, musically speaking, was devoted mostly to hip hop—honing in on Nas's 1994 masterpiece, *Illmatic*. With Michael Eric Dyson and Sohail Daulatzai's *Born to Use Mics* as our guide, we followed Nas's lyrical cartog-

---

[1] It is important to note that hip-hop culture, from its earliest days, has been more than simply MCs rapping over beat breaks produced by DJs. There are four "classical" elements of hip hop culture: (a) music produced by DJs via "sampling" on turntables; (b) rapping over the music by MCs, often in "freestyle battles"; (c) breakdancing to the music (again, often in a "battle" format); and (d) graffiti art (which also includes a competitive dimension). In this chapter, I am mostly interested in Tupac's raps and the graffiti-style art by "Riskie" on the cover for the *Makaveli* record. For a classic discussion of the development of hip hop culture in postindustrial New York, see Tricia Rose, *Black Noise: Rap Music and Black Culture in Contemporary America* (Middletown CT: Wesleyan University Press, 1994) 34–61.

[2] That year, Lamar was nominated for eleven GRAMMYs, winning three: in addition to Best Rap Album, he won Best Rap Performance and Best Rap Song for the track "Alright," which became the unofficial anthem of the Black Lives Matter movement. See Recording Academy, "Winners: 58th Annual GRAMMY Awards (2015)," *Recording Academy*, https://www.grammy.com/grammys/awards/58th-annual-grammy-awards.

raphy of the Queensbridge projects[3] to better understand the conditions that, to use Coates's term, *plunder* Black bodies.[4] While journeying with Nas was exciting, one difficulty in engaging in hip hop studies as a religion professor—even given the existence of the increasingly prolific field of studies in hip hop and religion[5]—was that I simply could not do justice to the poetics of Nas in particular and hip hop more broadly speaking. If, as Dyson suggests, Nas's *oeuvre* merits inclusion in the canon of American—indeed, world—literature, then it behooves anyone teaching on hip hop to help students learn to read Nas and his colleagues in the "game" for what the Russian Formalists call their "literariness."[6] It is precisely in the urban poets' ability to draw attention to the medium itself as "an autonomous source of pleasure" that words are made complex, drawing readers/listeners in even as those encountering the words find previous meanings made ambiguous.[7] This literary

---

[3] Daulatzai says, "On the vinyl pressing of *Illmatic*, the album is organized not by the typical Side A and Side B, but by '40th Side North' and '41st Side South,' the two streets that divide Nas's beloved Queensbridge, the largest housing project in the United States. By dividing the album in this way and centering Queensbridge, *Illmatic* becomes a sonic map, as the album serves as the legend for Nas's ghetto cartography, as he narrates his experiences and those who live in the Queensbridge housing projects." See Sohail Daulatzai, "Introduction: *Illmatic*: It Was Written," in Michael Eric Dyson and Sohail Daulatzai, eds., *Born to Use Mics: Reading Nas's* Illmatic (New York: Basic *Civitas* Books, 2010) 6.

[4] See, for instance, Ta-Nehisi Coates, *Between the World and Me* (New York: Spiegel & Grau, 2015) 21.

[5] See Monica R. Miller and Anthony B. Pinn, eds., *The Hip Hop and Religion Reader* (New York: Routledge, 2015); and Monica R. Miller, Anthony B. Pinn, and Bernard "Bun B" Freeman, eds., *Religion in Hip Hop: Mapping the New Terrain in the US* (New York: Bloomsbury, 2015).

[6] Victor Erlich, "Russian Formalism," in Alex Preminger and T.V. F. Brogan, eds., *The New Princeton Encyclopedia of Poetry and Poetics* (Princeton: Princeton University Press 1993) 1101.

[7] Erlich, "Russian Formalism."

approach, when combined with a hip hop and religion focus, arguably makes way for deeper understanding of the religious significance of various hip hop artifacts.

A colleague from the English department and I have been co-teaching a new interdisciplinary course that connects the poetic and religious dimensions of hip hop titled, "Word: Hip Hop, Religion, and Poetry."[8] We have found success by allowing particular hip hop (or hip hop-inspired) albums to serve as portals into understanding various religious traditions. Implicitly, ultimate concern forms a link between the albums and the religious traditions as we riff on the inherent tension Tillich recognized in the concept of "ultimate concern."[9] The religious traditions discussed in the course drive us toward the "ultimacy" of Tillich's ultimate concern, the albums listened to continuously bring students back to the concreteness of how we must feel, experience, or encounter ultimacy in existential concern.

This is a highly inductive process and for undergraduate students we have had to be more explicit about how to thematize ultimacy and existential concern. Thus, we have used categories provided by Stephen Prothero in *God Is Not One*. Prothero's "four-part approach to the [world] religions" analyzes each religion according to (a) the human problem it identifies; (b) the solution it finds to the problem; (c) the technique(s) it proposes for reaching the solution; and (d) those whom it identifies as exemplars of moving from problem to solution.[10] Providing these categories has

---

[8] This chapter is dedicated to my colleague, Dr. Marcus Hensel, and the students in our class, "Word: Hip Hop, Religion, and Poetry" (Fall 2017).

[9] Paul Tillich, *Systematic Theology*, 3 vols. (Chicago: University of Chicago Press, 1951–1963) 1:211.

[10] Stephen Prothero, *God Is Not One: The Eight Rival Religions that Run the World* (New York: HarperOne, 2010) 14.

precipitated the kind of inductive reasoning that allows for a nuanced appreciation of the ways in which the symbols of religious traditions—as manifest in the flows of MCs from Mos Def/Yasiin Bey to the RZA—enable marginalized people to, in the words of Tillich, "[experience] meaning within [their] desert of meaninglessness."[11] Methodologically, the iterations of these interdisciplinary courses have allowed me to develop a critical correlational method[12] for engaging hip hop that works not only at an introductory level for students but also as a way to generate scholarly discourse in a crucial but under-analyzed aspect of theologies of culture.

Because of his status as a cultural icon, as well as the availability of secondary literature on him, here I will engage the work of Tupac Amaru Shakur.[13] I will focus on the last album Shakur recorded before his death (and which was released just two months after his death), *The Don Killuminati: The 7 Day Theory*,[14] on

---

[11] Paul Tillich, *Theology of Culture* (New York: Oxford University Press, 1959) 75.

[12] Such a method is certainly amenable to Tillich's method of correlation, though reflects elements of David Tracy's hermeneutical approach to correlational theology as well. See Tillich, *Systematic Theology*, 1:34–68; and David Tracy, *The Analogical Imagination* (New York: Crossroad Publishing, 1981) ch. 2–4.

[13] In this chapter, I will refer to the late rapper alternately as "Tupac," "Shakur," "Pac," "2Pac," and "Makaveli," not only for the sake of variation, but also to mirror the myriad ways in which both 'Pac referred to himself and others name(d) him.

[14] Makaveli, *The Don Killuminati: The 7 Day Theory* (Los Angeles: Death Row/Interscope, 1996). On the album's release, see Rob Marriott, "End of Discussion: Why 2Pac's 'The Don Killuminati: The 7 Day Theory' Is Better Than 'All Eyez On Me," *Complex*, last modified November 6, 2011, http://www.complex.com/music/2011/11/end-of-discussion-2pac-don-killuminati-the-7-day-theory-is-better-than-all-eyez-on-me/. On the significance of 2Pac's Makavelian moniker, the album's title, and theories about the meaning of "The 7 Day Theory," see Anthony B. Pinn and Paul Easter-

which 'Pac rapped as the alias "Makaveli," an allusion to the six-teenth-century political philosopher responsible for *The Prince*. A main reason for the selection of this album is its cover art by Ronald "Riskie" Brent, in which Shakur is depicted hanging on a cross, and the titles and content of songs like "Hail Mary" and "Blasphemy." The second verse to "Blasphemy" alone could suffice for a succinct primer on the relevance of traditional Christian sto-ries and symbols for the Black church, albeit framed within 'Pac's "thugged-out" imagination.

Shakur's modes of self-signification, including the image of his body hanging on the cross and vivid imagery of his lyrics, func-tion *symbolically*. Tillich's understanding of symbols in *Dynamics of Faith* can help to illuminate the symbolic expressions of pain and suffering of Black (male) bodies in the age of mass incarceration through hip hop. I am not proposing anything novel by suggesting that Tupac is a symbol, religious or otherwise. Indeed, it is fasci-nating how often Shakur is described in symbolic terms in Dyson's *Holler If You Hear Me*.[15] This chapter will frame the symbolic sig-nificance of 2Pac in explicitly Tillichian terms, however, by engag-ing *Dynamics of Faith*, *Theology of Culture*, and *Courage to Be*. Do-ing so will deepen the appreciation of Shakur's religio-cultural relevance, extend the aesthetic dimensions of Tillich's work on culture to the artistic category of hip hop,[16] and foster a deeper

---

ling, "Followers of Black Jesus on Alert: Thoughts on the Story of Tupac Shakur's Life/Death/Life," in *Black Theology: An International Journal* 7/1 (2009): 39. All songs dealt with in this chapter are from the *Makaveli* album. Therefore, I will not provide full references for them in the footnotes.

[15] See, for example, Michael Eric Dyson, *Holler If You Hear Me: Search-ing for Tupac Shakur* (New York: Basic *Civitas* Books, 2001) 149, 159, 233, 244, 252, and 265–66.

[16] Margarita L. Simon Guillory does engage Tillich's understanding of the erotic in "Intersecting Points: The 'Erotic as Religious' in the Lyrics of Missy Elliott," in Miller and Pinn, *The Hip Hop and Religion Reader*, 102–

sense of courage in the face of the realities Shakur so vividly describes in his raps.

THUG LIFE/CRUCIFORM LIFE

In *Dynamics of Faith*, Tillich offers his classic discussion of symbols, naming six particular characteristics.[17] For the purposes of this chapter, I am primarily interested in the third characteristic, "that it opens up levels of reality which otherwise are closed for us."[18] Tillich goes on to say the arts "create symbols for a level of reality which cannot be reached in any other way."[19] Tillich predominately engages the visual arts,[20] but his insight may apply equally to music, and more particularly to hiphop culture and music. To return briefly to the previous appeal to Russian Formalism and "literariness," one could say that by "defamiliarizing" language for its listeners,[21] hip hop opens up levels of reality otherwise unreachable, particularly those levels marked by grotesquerie. Thus, even as its symbolism is more explicitly representational (e.g., Tupac's being depicted on a cross on the *Makaveli* album cover and explicitly referring to the media's crucifixion of "brothers"), its play with language nonetheless provides new vistas for understanding

---

114; yet there is still remaining a dearth of work of thoroughly Tillichian analyses of hip hop.

[17] Paul Tillich, *Dynamics of Faith* (New York: Harper, 1957) 47–50.

[18] Ibid., 48.

[19] Ibid.

[20] Note the attention Tillich pays to Pablo Picasso's "Guernica" in the chapter "Protestantism and Artistic Style," found in *Theology of Culture*, 68–75. See also Russell Re Manning's comments in "The Religious Meaning of Culture: Paul Tillich and Beyond," *International Journal of Systematic Theology* 15/4 (October 2013): 444–45.

[21] In referring to "defamiliarization," I am drawing on Victor Shklovsky, "Art as Technique," in David H. Richter, ed., *The Critical Tradition: Classic Texts and Contemporary Trends*, 3rd ed. (Boston and New York: Bedford/St. Martin's, 2006) 774–84.

old signifiers.

To show how Tupac's stigmatized body functions as a religious symbol, I first suggest how 'Pac's body functions as a symbol more generally according to Tillich's third characteristic. I then show how his symbolism is intensified by taking an explicitly cruciform shape. I first speak to the ways in which Shakur's body—in its tattooed visual appearance and in the various activities in which it is said to be engaged on *The Don Killuminati: The 7 Day Theory*—provides vistas for understanding the experience of the Black (male) body in America. The various meanings of Tupac's "thug life" ideology are significant for this discussion. Indeed, "thug life" may serve as a heuristic for exploring the symbolic significance of Tupac's body at the end of his life and in his death.

Second, I speak to the ways in which this embodied symbolism explicitly merges itself with classical Christian symbols, rendering Tupac's stigmatized body a religious symbol. In particular, I examine the cover art for *The Don Killuminati: The 7 Day Theory*, specific lyrics on the album, and the posthumous reception and interpretation of Tupac's body (of work).

Finally, in the constructive section of the chapter, I draw upon Tillich's ontology of courage in *The Courage to Be* to suggest that, in becoming sin on behalf of his "thug nation," Tupac both epitomizes and symbolizes "the universal and essential self-affirmation of one's being"[22] in the Black (male) community. It is precisely his *courage to be* in the face of the harsh and negative realities of the American ghetto and penitentiary that lend his body such symbolic significance. Further, I look toward a future in which, because all symbols must eventually die, 'Pac's body may cease to be a symbol of the brutality experienced in Black-

---

[22] Paul Tillich, *The Courage to Be*, 2nd ed. (New Haven: Yale University Press, 2000) 3.

American life and instead become the symbol of resurrection.

"IT'S THE CITY OF ANGELS, IN CONSTANT DANGER": THE PRESENCE OF THE ULTIMATE IN THE GROTESQUE REALITIES OF THE GHETTO

In *Holler If You Hear Me*, Michael Eric Dyson poignantly describes Shakur's complexly interpreted body as "beautiful, tattooed, wounded, conflicted, drugged, lurching, representative, fighting, cursing, defiant, loving, needy, sacrificial."[23] The body of the slain rapper is rife with symbolic significance for those for whom he died. "…Tupac's bullet-riddled body is an unavoidable symbol of the rage and murder that destroy precious black bodies."[24] In his life, Tupac's own recognition of this symbolic significance is evident in the tattooed discourse inscribed on his body, on which he bears a kind of hypostatic union of the symbols dear to the Black church on the one hand, and those associated with gangsta rap and thug life on the other. It's almost as if in the inscriptions on his material body, he anticipates the transfiguration of his status, which his discursive body will annunciate *postmortem*.[25]

Thinking of two tattoos in particular will suffice for a brief consideration of the union of religious and thug symbols on Tupac's body. First, covering most of his back is a large cross. Inscribed within the cross is "EXODUS," and "1831" is tattooed just below the letters. While some, such as Dyson,[26] interpret the numbers as "18:11,"[27] referring to a specific verse from Exodus,[28]

---

[23] Dyson, *Holler If You Hear Me*, 246.

[24] Ibid., 233.

[25] I am drawing the distinction between material and discursive bodies from Anthony Pinn, *Embodiment and the New Shape of Black Theological Thought* (New York: NYU Press, 2010).

[26] Dyson, *Holler If You Hear Me*, 232.

[27] They do so because there is no Exodus 18:31.

[28] Exodus 18:11 reads, "Now I know that the LORD is greater than all

others read the numbers more straightforwardly as "1831," referring to the year of the Nat Turner-led slave rebellion in South-
ampton County, Virginia.[29] Visual evidence would seem to point
to the latter interpretation. In that case, Tupac is linking the central symbol of Christianity (the cross) to both the biblical book
most associated with the tradition of the Black church (Exodus)[30]
and the event that is symbolic of the necessity of a literal exodus
out of slavery for those shackled in America (Nat Turner's rebellion). Whereas in the case of his tattooing, Tupac inscribes a cross
on his body, he later places his own body on a cross in a remarka-
ble aesthetic depiction of his inevitable martyrdom.[31]

Perhaps the most iconic of Tupac's tattoos is the arc-shaped
phrase "THUG LIFE," spread across his abdomen. Notably, in
the script of the word "LIFE," a vertically arranged bullet replaces
the "I."[32] In case onlookers may otherwise be unconvinced by his
stated commitment to thug life, the tattoos on the front of his torso are interspersed with scars from actual bullet wounds.[33] In a
comparison of the textual articulations of the despised bodies of
both Jesus the Christ and Tupac, Anthony Pinn and Paul Easter-

---

gods, because he delivered the people from the Egyptians, when they dealt
arrogantly with them" (NRSV). It is possible that Tupac meant to quote
Exodus 18:11, but mistakenly had "1831" tattooed within the cross instead.

[29] Nick Grant, "The Tattoos of 2Pac, Decoded," *Complex*, last modified
13 September 2016, www.complex.com/style/2016/09/2pac-tattoos-
decoded.

[30] See Allen Dwight Callahan, *The Talking Book: African Americans and
the Bible* (New Haven: Yale University Press, 2006) 83.

[31] On Tupac's martyrdom, see Dyson, *Holler If You Hear Me*, 264–68.

[32] Grant, "The Tattoos of 2Pac, Decoded."

[33] Dyson notes, "Tupac served eleven months in jail after being convict-
ed in a 1994 sexual assault of a woman in a New York hotel room. During
his trial he was shot five times in what appeared to be an armed-robbery attempt in New York's Quad Recording Studios" (*Holler If You Hear Me*, 169–
70).

ling draw a crucial distinction: "…unlike Christian scripture, Tu-pac provides a 'sacred' word carved into the despised Black body—in this way highlighting the centrality and significance of the body—the tattoo. Central to this presentation of the word in flesh is 'thug life' written across his body, the fundamental framework of the life stance he promotes."[34] Pinn and Easterling go on to sug-gest that those who "mark their bodies with signs and symbols related to their devotion [to Tupac], experience a stigmata—i.e., they are participating in the pain and pleasure 'preached' by Tupac through markings of Tupac's realness, even in his absence."[35] Re-cently, NBA All-Star Kevin Durant made the news when he had such a stigmatic experience, getting a large tattoo of Tupac's face on his left leg.[36] So what is "thug life" and what about it is so sig-nificant for those who follow the fallen rapper?

Having a knack for acronyms,[37] Shakur succinctly defines "thug life" thus: "The Hate U Gave Little Infants Fucks Every-body."[38] In an interview with MTV, Tupac elaborates this mean-ing, saying, "It's not thugging like I'm robbing people, 'cause that's not what I'm doing…I mean, like, I'm not scared to say how I feel. Part of being [a thug] is to stand up for your responsibility and say this is what I do even though I know people are going to hate

---

[34] Pinn and Easterling, "Followers of Black Jesus on Alert," 36–37.

[35] Ibid., 37.

[36] Eduardo Gonzalez, "Kevin Durant shows off his new Tupac tattoo," *Los Angeles Times*, last modified 22 July 2016, http://www.latimes.com/sports/sportsnow/la-sp-kevin-durant-shows-off-new-tupac-tattoo-20160722-snap-htmlstory.html.

[37] To name just one other example, Tupac interprets the slang term "nigga" acronymically with "never ignorant, getting goals accomplished" (Dy-son, *Holler If You Hear Me*, 144).

[38] Michael P. Jeffries, "Can a Thug (get some) Love? Sex, Romance, and the Definition of a Hip-Hop 'Thug,'" *Women and Language*, 32/2 (2009): 36.

me…"[39] If, in *Holler If You Hear Me,* Dyson helpfully narrates Tupac's psychological trauma and transformations across the many trajectories of his short life, Pinn, in *Embodiment and the New Shape of Black Theological Thought,* digs more deeply into the late rapper's thug responsibility, suggesting that his full embrace of all that was entailed in thug life is indicative of a conversion.[40] Describing such a conversion moves us closer to the symbolic significance of 'Pac's body.

Noting the rapper's own claim that his music is "spiritual,"[41] Pinn draws important similarities and differences between Tupac's thug spirituality and that of the Black church. Shakur and the Black church hold in common a recognition of the absurdity of the world experienced by people of color in America. However, Tupac differs from the Black church in his response to the world's absurdity. Whereas the conversion process typical in the Black church "problematiz[es] engagement [with] the world," Tupac— in some ways bearing similarities to Albert Camus's approach to absurdity in *The Myth of Sisyphus*[42] and features of biblical wisdom literature—presses himself more fully into the world by transform-

---

[39] Quoted in Dyson, *Holler If You Hear Me,* 113.

[40] Pinn, *Embodiment and the New Shape of Black Theological Thought,* 131.

[41] Tupac says his "music is spiritual, if you listen to it… It's all about emotion; it's all about life" (quoted in ibid.).

[42] Albert Camus, *The Myth of Sisyphus and Other Essays,* trans. Justin O'Brien (New York: Alfred A. Knopf, 1955). For a fascinating correspondence between Camusian absurdity and biblical wisdom, particularly Ecclesiastes, see Michael V. Fox, *A Time to Tear Down and a Time to Build Up: A Rereading of Ecclesiastes* (Grand Rapids: William B. Eerdmans Publishing Company, 1999). In connection with the present chapter, Pinn has also detected linkages between Camusian absurdity and hip hop. See Anthony B. Pinn, "Zombies in the Hood: Rap music, Camusian absurdity, and the structuring of death," in Miller, Pinn, and Freeman, *Religion in Hip Hop,* 183–97.

ing himself into a "thug." Elsewhere, I have pointed out the ways in which the German reformer, Martin Luther, revolutionized the reading of Ecclesiastes precisely by reading it as something of a manual for everyday economic and political life. Ecclesiastes, according to Luther, doesn't call one away from worldly concern, but pushes one further into earthly vocations, as activity in the muck and mire of quotidian existence is for Luther a *locus* of encounter with God through the various creaturely masks (*larvae Dei*) through which God communicates with God's people.[43] If Luther's understanding of the thrust of biblical wisdom—evident in his lectures on both Ecclesiastes and Song of Songs—is taken seriously, we may understand Tupac's thug conversion as a kind of anti-monastic, non-pious, Ecclesiastan push into quotidian life, with all its vicissitudes and relationships and ambiguity.

Pinn describes Tupac's wisdom turn thus: "In this way, conversion does not mean disengagement from the world or an effort to purge the si(g)ns of worldly involvement, but rather a more energetic engagement *with* the world."[44] Concomitant with this conversion is an "epistemological shift" that recognizes "the beauty within the grotesque" and "an alternate valuation of those things stigmatized or picked out for greater monitoring because of their difference."[45] In 'Pac's new epistemological posture, "[t]he divine is embedded in the despised—or thug—modalities and aesthetic of life."[46] Thus, one need not "fly away" to heaven to enter into the presence of the divine, but rather may live more fully in recogni-

---

[43] For a full treatment of Luther's Ecclesiastes lectures, see Tyler Atkinson, *Singing at the Winepress: Ecclesiastes and the Ethics of Work* (London; New York: T&T Clark, 2015) 121–85.

[44] Pinn, *Embodiment and the New Shape of Black Theological Thought*, 131.

[45] Ibid., 131–32.

[46] Ibid., 132.

tion of the presence of the divine within the everyday and grotesque realities of the ghetto.

Tupac's body is symbolic of the experience of the Black (male) body in America in the way described by Pinn: body modifications through tattooing are a means to subvert the surveillance tactics of America's (in)justice system such that "the stigmatized body is given unapologetic visibility, and the monitoring of that body is turned on its head: surveillance meant to control becomes a source of defiance."[47] If the hate directed toward the children of the ghetto indeed "fucks everybody," then Tupac's vengeful "Fuck you!" to the world,[48] expressed in the inked modifications to his body, symbolizes both his people's plight and their resistance to white America's perception and plunder of their bodies. Not content to wear his ideology on his body, however, Shakur also expresses such ideology in his music, especially the album *The Don Killuminati: The 7 Day Theory*.

On the *Makaveli* record, 'Pac positions himself as both the archetype and the scapegoat of thug life. Functioning as something of a meta-critical thread connecting the album's songs and the various subthemes of thug life is what Dyson calls a "culture of death," in which "[t]he dead black body…is so common as to become a metaphor itself: Suffering black flesh is the window onto the spiritual trauma that afflicts an entire generation."[49] In hip hop, argues Dyson, the autopsy of Black bodies is a rhetorical device, leading to a proliferation of eulogies and other expressions of

---

[47] Pinn, *Embodiment and the New Shape of Black Theological Thought*, 132.

[48] In a description of Tupac's tattoos, Dyson notes, "'Fuck the World' ran across his trapezoids; the same phrase, this time in script, ran across his shoulder blades" (*Holler If You Hear Me*, 132).

[49] Ibid., 226.

mourning.[50] Such a move shows up in the Makaveli song "To Live and Die in L.A.," in which he rhymes, "Shed tears as we bury niggas close to heart / What was a friend now a ghost in the dark."[51] Death is mourned again both in "White Man'z World" ("Bein' born with less, I must confess, only adds on to the stress / Two shots to my homie's head, died in his vest / Shot him to death and left him bleedin' for his family to see / I pass his casket gently askin', 'Is there heaven for Gs?'") and in "Blasphemy" (where Makaveli prays, "Dear Lord, don't let me die tonight").

The culture of death that animates Tupac's lyrics not only functions as a metacritique, but also is indicative of the particular places in which he and his homies find themselves: the penitentiary and the ghetto. The many realities surrounding the prison industrial complex[52] and the mass incarceration[53] of young Black males—including police profiling, brutality towards people of color, and severe sentencing as a result of the "War on Drugs" and "tough on crime" policies—are topics of concern on *The Don Killuminati: The 7 Day Theory*.[54] On "Blasphemy," 'Pac is worried that

---

[50] Ibid., 228.

[51] Quoted in ibid., 229.

[52] For a full description of what is entailed in the term "prison industrial complex," see Angela Y. Davis, *Are Prisons Obsolete?* (New York: Seven Stories Press, 2003) 85–104. For a discussion of the effects of the prison industrial complex on the families of incarcerated Black males, see Earl Smith and Angela J. Hattery, "African-American Men and the Prison Industrial Complex," *Western Journal of Black Studies* 34/4 (2010): 387–98.

[53] Mass incarceration, according to Michelle Alexander, "refers not only to the criminal justice system but also to the larger web of laws, rules, policies, and customs that control those labeled criminals both in and out of prison." See Michelle Alexander, *The New Jim Crow: Mass Incarceration in the Age of Colorblindness*, rev. ed. (New York: The New Press, 2012) 13.

[54] Note, for instance, the allusion to Bill Clinton's 1994 Crime Bill in "To Live and Die in L.A.": "So many niggas gettin' three strikes, tossed in jail / I swear the pen right across from hell."

even God might be "another cop" strolling through "this crime land" and looking to punish citizens of 'Pac's beloved "thug nation." The second verse of "Hail Mary" notably describes the effect of the prison industrial complex on the Black (male) psyche: "Penitentiaries is packed with promise makers / Never realize the precious time the bitch niggas is wastin' / Institutionalized, I lived my life, a product made to crumble / But too hardened for a smile, we're too crazy to be humble."[55] Makaveli goes on to say, "I got a head with no screws in it. What can I do? / One life to live, but I got nothin' to love. Just me and you / On a one-way trip to prison, sellin' drugs / We all wrapped up in this livin', life as thugs." There is an inescapability from the cycle between illicit vocations for the sake of flourishing and the Black (male) body being pressed again into the machinations of the prison industrial complex. This inevitability has a profound effect on 2Pac's own experience.

Dyson goes at length to show that 2Pac's eleven-month prison stay left an indelible mark on 'Pac, inspiring a fatalistic and self-destructive commitment not simply to portray thug life in his music, but also to become its very embodiment.[56] And yet, becoming such an embodiment of thug life unto the point of death—even death by a gunshot—is perhaps for Shakur a means of "becoming sin" on behalf of his "thug nation," that they might "thug eternal." The conclusion of the second verse to "Hail Mary" intimates such an idea: "To my homeboys in Quentin Max doin' they bid / Raise hell to this real shit, and feel this / When they turn out the lights, I'll be there in the dark / Thuggin' eternal through my heart. Now Hail Mary, nigga." Here, Tupac intimates a sense of his real presence to his homeboys even after his death. Already, we

---

[55] I am indebted to my colleague, Marcus Hensel, for the transcription of "Hail Mary."

[56] Dyson, *Holler If You Hear Me*, 212–16.

are touching on the religious significance of his body, in his life and after his death. Before addressing this in detail, we must consider that other grotesque environment, namely the ghetto, which is indicative of the culture of death animated in his lyrics.

Tupac's vision of ghetto life can be seen in the dialectic between the consecutively tracked songs "To Live and Die in L.A." and "Blasphemy." The former observes daily life in Los Angeles ghettos ("Cost me more to be free than the life in the pen / Makin' money offa cuss words writin' again"), and the latter places the ghetto in a more explicitly metaphysical context ("We probly in hell already," "Have you ever seen a crackhead? That's eternal fire").[57] Such a claim is reinforced by the ways in which, in the mixing and mastering of the record, "To Live and Die in L.A." bleeds into the introduction of "Blasphemy." Here a presenter from the Christian television program *This Week in Bible Prophecy* proclaims that God has a perfect plan and that accepting the Christ as one's personal lord and savior ensures one's ability to be a part of that perfect plan. Further, there is an apocalyptic anticipation of the Christ's return, which adds to the urgency of the call to accept the Christ, lest one is lost forever. Given the importance of the number seven for this album, from the title to the number of gunshots heard in "Bomb First,"[58] it is significant that the sample from *This Week in Bible Prophecy* includes the concluding statement, "Unless the Lord does return in the coming seven days, we'll

---

[57] This is not to ignore the equation of the ghetto with hell in "To Live and Die in L.A.," in such lines as "What's the worst they can do to a nigga, got me lost in hell / To live and die in L.A. on bail." Rather, the invocation of God in "Blasphemy" (such as the recitation of the Lord's Prayer at the end of the song) places 'Pac's observations within a more strictly metaphysical framework. Yet, in so doing, he renders problematic any notion that hell is something experienced in the hereafter and not the now.

[58] Pinn and Easterling, "Followers of Black Jesus on Alert," 39.

see you next time here on *This Week in Bible Prophecy.*" The message of the presenter is intensified by the vocal effect added to the sample, wherein, if one is listening in stereo, the left speaker presents the presenter's actual voice, but in the right speaker the voice sounds monstrous, demonic even.

Immediately following the sample, Shakur urges himself, "Tupac, don't start that blasphemy." Given the ecclesial hypocrisy 2Pac describes in the third verse of "Blasphemy," it seems that the rhetorical function of sampling the Christian television presenter is to problematize the casting of judgment toward the lifestyles described in "To Live and Die in L.A." and to vindicate such lifestyles as responses to the absurdities of ghetto life. Surely, Jesus, "a kind man," would be empathetic toward those on the underside of the American dream and the empty sermon. In other words, Tupac takes issue with Christian preachers and teachers (like those on shows such as *This Week in Bible Prophecy*) who urge people to turn from their (L.A.) ways, while ignoring the harsh realities that might lead one to follow that "little bit of thug in 'em." Furthermore, teachers and preachers ignore the fact that the "ass-kissin'" taking place in churches is a form of escapism, if not the exploitation of Black suffering for the sake of the material comforts of the minister. Why can't a thug have such material comforts, whatever the means of finding it?

In response to the absurdities of life in the ghetto and the penitentiary, Makaveli plunges himself into those bodily activities and acquisitive behaviors that help to anaesthetize Black (male) suffering: getting money, having sexual intercourse, taking drugs (particularly marijuana) and alcohol ('Pac has a taste for Hennessey), and enacting violence. The opening track of the *Makaveli* album, "Bomb First (My Second Reply)," contains a succinct summary of 'Pac's embrace of the material(ism): "West coast rida, comin' right behind ya / Shoulda never fucked with me / I want money, hoes, sex, and weed." Throughout the remainder of the album, different tracks epitomize particular material themes. For instance, "Toss It Up" and "Just Like Daddy" celebrate thug sexuality in explicit terms, while "Life of an Outlaw" and "Me and My Girlfriend" (in which "girlfriend" is a metaphor for 'Pac's gun) speak to the wrath and vengeance the rapper wishes to enact on his rivals. Furthermore, the hook to "Krazy" ("Time goes by, puffin' no lie / Hopin' that it gets me high /Got a nigga goin' crazy / I feel crazy") refers to the pleasures of smoking marijuana (Tupac's consumption of Hennessey is also mentioned in the song), while "Blasphemy" contains the axiomatic acronym "M.O.B.," which stands for "money over bitches." For Shakur, to rap so explicitly is both to vindicate and to symbolize a way of life that functions as a response to ghetto grotesquerie precisely by participating in those acts deemed immoral by the wider culture, but made inescapable by the realities surrounding the prison industrial complex.

It should be evident by now that Makaveli lays out a lifestyle for the thug that is indicative of the rage and sense of absurdity experienced by Black males in the ghetto and the penitentiary. Furthermore, I've tried to illustrate the ways in which Makaveli himself symbolizes that ideology, the ways of being thug in America. I move now to link such symbolic work to Tillich's notion of cultural artifacts' ability to locate the ultimate in the ugly experiences of reality, in the grotesque.

In his brief chapter "Protestantism and Artistic Style," found in *Theology of Culture*, Tillich articulates what provides art its religious significance, namely, its realistic depictions of ultimate concern precisely in the divine-demonic dialectic operative in the negative shadow side of everything that exists.[59] Operating from the perspective of a Lutheran *theologia crucis*, Protestant art tends not to focus on resurrection glory so much as cruciform suffering.[60] Insofar as it provides access to the presence of the divine-demonic in ugly realities inaccessible to the non-aesthetic perception, art has a unique vocation in terms of the expression of ultimate concern.

If we apply Tillich's understanding of Protestant art to Tupac's bodily inscriptions and the poetics of his raps, we find for Pablo Picasso a striking musical partner. In his expressions of "thug life," rife as they are with presentations of the Black (male) body as subject of ultimate concern, Tupac employs precisely and explicitly the divine-demonic dialectic (heard, for instance, in the stereo effects added to the sample from the Christian presenter at the beginning of "Blasphemy") to draw attention to the American underside, to grotesquerie. Just as witnesses of visual art experience an inclination simultaneously to look toward and turn their faces away from depictions of the negative, so, too, are listeners of the *Makaveli* record drawn to the emotions of 'Pac's lyrical delivery, even as they perhaps recoil from the sound of gunshots or threats upon the lives of 'Pac's various opponents. But it is precisely this existential tension that reveals the dialectic contained within Shakur's body (of work) to be symbolic of ghetto grotesquerie. What comes to intensify his body's religious-symbolic significance is the merging of the symbols of thug life with the symbols associated with the Christ, especially the cross.

---

[59] Tillich, *Theology of Culture*, 73.
[60] Ibid., 75.

"PLUS THE MEDIA BE CRUCIFYIN' BROTHERS SEVERELY": THE PRESENCE OF THE NEGATIVE IN THE SYMBOL OF THE CROSS

Towards the conclusion of his short chapter on Protestant art, Tillich draws attention to the particular religious symbols taken up (or not) by artists. The cross of the Christ is utilized often in the style associated with Picasso (Cubism), says Tillich, but importantly, there is yet to be a symbolic representation of resurrection in Protestant art. According to Tillich, this dearth in resurrection symbolism is a good thing, as prematurely symbolizing resurrection would imply a forfeiture of the courageous expression of "the human situation in its conflicts" that cruciform symbolism provides.[61] The way to meaning vis-à-vis meaninglessness is precisely to "bear and express meaninglessness."[62] So long as the human situation is marked by despair, there must remain an existential preference for an artistic *theologia crucis*. Yes, symbols must die,[63] but not before the tragic contexts to which they draw our gaze and our ears have dissipated.

Like Cubism, in its visual-artistic dimensions, hip hop has an affinity for drawing attention to human conflict through the symbolism of the cross. Admittedly, hip hop does so often through more explicitly representational means (i.e., by placing its rap icons upon obvious crosses) and thus risks compromising the depth dimension in the third characteristic of the symbol for Tillich. Yet, perhaps by explicitly placing black men on the cross of the Christ—who in predominantly white churches is often depicted as white—such explicitness is exactly what is needed to lure the potentially offended into the depths of the broken realities of Black

---

[61] Ibid.
[62] Ibid.
[63] Tillich, *Dynamics of Faith*, 49–50.

life in America. Rappers from Kanye West[64] to Nas[65] have invoked the cross to infuse their rhymes with deeper symbolic significance. Arguably, none have done so quite as profoundly as Tupac Shakur. In so doing, he follows in the footsteps of those theologians who have identified people of color in America as the "crucified people." Thus, before directing our eyes to the cover art of the *Makaveli* album and our ears to the lyrics of "Blasphemy" as moving toward an expression of courage as with Tillich, we must draw some connections between the work of James Cone and that of 2Pac.

In his haunting and powerful book *The Cross and the Lynching Tree*, James Cone suggests that one cannot understand Christian identity in America unless one learns to read the cross of the Christ and the lynching tree as mutually interpreting symbols.[66] Cone reflects on the power of Black art in its use of symbols to

---

[64] Note the second version of the music video for West's "Jesus Walks," in which scenes involving a modern-day chain gang—comprised of African American men monitored by white officers—are interspersed with an unfolding scene of a Klansman constructing a cross from a tree. Significantly, in one of the chain-gang scenes, a prisoner is patted down and searched by an officer, taking a cruciform shape while being harassed by the officer. To return to the other scene mentioned, upon completion of cross construction, the Klansman sets the cross on fire; however, the cross falls and begins to tumble down a hill. In "rescuing" the tumbling cross, its builder is engulfed in flames as well. See Kanye West, "Kanye West—Jesus Walks (Version 2)," video, 4:06, 24 December 2009, https://www.youtube.com/watch?v=MY-F7H_fpc-g.

[65] See Nas, "Nas—Hate Me Now ft. Puff Daddy," video, 5:17, 25 October 2009, https://www.youtube.com/watch?v=dKSJN3WWR3E, in which Nas himself is depicted on a cross. For a treatment of this video, see Siphiwe Ignatius Dube, "Hate Me Now: An Instance of NAS as Hip-Hop's Self-Proclaimed Prophet and Messiah," in Miller and Pinn, *The Hip Hop and Religion Reader*, 377–91.

[66] James H. Cone, *The Cross and the Lynching Tree* (Maryknoll NY: Orbis Books, 2011) 161.

provide depth dimensions for understanding the Black-American experience of suffering, in order to lay claim to what Cone calls their "somebodiness."[67] From blues musicians to the poets of the Harlem Renaissance, Black artists have invoked religious symbols both to interpret and to draw attention to the harsh realities of the lynching of Black bodies, the practice of which continues—if not with nooses and trees—with police brutality and mass incarceration.[68] Billie Holiday's performance of "Strange Fruit" does for Cone what Picasso's "Guernica" does for Tillich, namely, provides access to dimensions of suffering and grotesquerie otherwise inaccessible to majority hearers/viewers. Through the sheer emotion of her performance of Abel Meeropol's poem, Holiday communicates the cries of the crucified. What the blues does for Cone, so hip hop does for succeeding generations. Indeed, multiple hip hop artists have in their own ways riffed on Holiday's legendary performance.[69]

Scholars such as Pinn have made important connections between the ethos of the blues and that of hip hop. According to Pinn, gangsta rappers in particular could be called "children of the blues," as they "share many of the existential commitments and the moral sensibilities of the blues performers, and this includes a similar stance on lived synergy between demonic forces and rebel-

---

[67] Ibid., 14.

[68] Note the chapter, "Seeing Jesus in Michael Brown: New Theological Constructions of Blackness," in Rima Vesely-Flad, *Racial Purity and Dangerous Bodies: Moral Pollution, Black Lives, and the Struggle for Justice* (Minneapolis: Fortress Press, 2017) 175–94.

[69] For instance, Lupe Fiasco, "Strange Fruition" (featuring Casey Benjamin), *Food and Liquor II: The Great American Rap Album Pt. 1* (Los Angeles: Atlantic Records, Sept. 2012); Kanye West, "Blood on the Leaves," *Yeezus* (New York: Def Jam Recordings, June 2013); and Common, "Letter to the Free" (featuring Bilal), *Black America Again* (New York: Def Jam Recordings, Nov. 2016).

lious humans."[70] Therefore, it is fitting to connect Cone's comments regarding the ability of the blues to communicate deeply the horrors of lynching-as-crucifixion to hip-hop music, particularly the work of Tupac. Like Billie Holiday and Countee Cullen before him, Shakur detects a resonance between Black suffering in America and the suffering of the Christ on the cross. Katie Grimes has gone as far to call 'Pac a "theologian of the crucified people," suggesting "Tupac crafts a theological aesthetics of liberation aimed at illuminating the injustice and Christological implications of the hyper-segregated ghetto and the black mass prison. As such, Tupac's music sounds like a modern-day Psalm 22 and Song of Suffering Servanthood."[71] If Grimes builds upon Dyson's naming of 'Pac as a "ghetto saint," I wish here to build upon Grimes by suggesting 'Pac is not only a "theologian of the crucified people," but in his own stigmatic experience becomes the crucified one, the quintessential symbol of all crucifixions of Black bodies in America. Thus, he is symbolically not only martyr, saint, prophet, and theologian, but also Christ. We shall soon see that after his death, he indeed becomes venerated and worshiped as the Christ. Shakur himself seems to anticipate such veneration in his request to be depicted on a cross in the cover art for the Makaveli album.

The cover art of *The Don Killuminati: The 7 Day Theory* features a graffiti-style airbrush painting of Tupac hanging on a cross. In an interview with Michael Namikas of HipHopDX.com, Death Row Records album cover artist Ronald "Riskie" Brent relays that 2Pac wanted Riskie to paint him on a cross for the cover.

---

[70] Pinn, *Embodiment and the New Shape of Black Theological Thought*, 113.

[71] Katie Grimes, "'But Do the Lord Care?': Tupac Shakur as Theologian of the Crucified People," in *Political Theology* 15/4 (2014): 327.

When Riskie showed 'Pac the unfinished canvas, in which the cross has not yet been filled in, the rapper asked, "Yo, can you make the cross into a road map?"[72] Shakur then told Riskie which cities he wanted on the map, cities he felt had crucified him in one way or another. He also "wanted a compass on top of it to signify east to west. The compass was real important to him."[73] Thus, the Makavelian crucifixion features Tupac hanging on a cross with a bandana (his signature headwear) laden with thorns for a crown, gunshot wounds and a wounded side interspersed with tattoos, and the parental advisory sticker placed across his groin area. The various maps on the cross include the five boroughs of New York City (as well as East Orange, NJ) to the "east," with California cities Oakland, Hollywood, Southcentral Los Angeles, Watts, Compton, and Long Beach not on the far western end of the horizontal crossbeam, but rather at the crossing, above Tupac's head. At the far northern part of the cross is the east-west compass, with Midwestern cities Detroit and Chicago listed just below. Various southern cities are listed on the cross behind Shakur's torso and buttocks, but not in their geographical order: from top to bottom are New Orleans, Atlanta, Houston, and Dallas. Riskie showed the finished painting to Shakur the evening before the latter was fatally shot in Las Vegas. Shakur "loved it" and "raved about it."[74] Perhaps such love for the art is indicative of the crucifixion's faithful iconizing of the album's musical content, especially the second verse to "Blasphemy," in which Tupac most explicitly connects himself to the narrative of the Christ.

---

[72] Michael Namikas, "Makaveli & Riskie: A Conversation with Death Row Graphic Artist Ronald 'Riskie' Brent," *HipHopDX*, last modified 5 November 2015, https://hiphopdx.com/interviews/id.2807/title.makaveli-riskie-a-conversation-with-death-row-graphic-artist-ronald-riskie-brent#.

[73] Namikas, "Makaveli & Riskie."

[74] Ibid.

I have already discussed the introduction to the song "Blasphemy" in its connection to "To Live and Die in L.A." Here, I wish to focus on just the second verse to show the ways in which Shakur identifies with the Christ, after making connections to other moments in salvation history. Throughout the verse, 'Pac maps the realities of the ghetto onto biblical narratives, especially Exodus (and thus following the tradition of the Black church). For instance, Makaveli spits, "They say Moses split the Red Sea / I split a blunt and rolled a fat one up deadly / Babylon beware, comin' for the Pharaoh's kids / Retaliation makin' legends off the shit we did." What is most significant for our purposes is the direct connection to both the infancy narratives and the crucifixion of the Christ: "Put my soul on it; I'm fightin' devil niggas daily / Plus the media be crucifyin' brothers severely / Tell me I ain't God's son; nigga, Mama a virgin / We got evicted, had to leave the 'burbs, back in the ghetto." 2Pac connects the thug story to the crucifixion in a general way ("Plus the media be crucifyin' brothers severely") before identifying himself with the Christ vis-à-vis the infancy narratives. He refers explicitly to the virgin birth before seeming to allude to the flight of the Holy Family to Egypt when he refers to his own family's eviction from the suburbs back to the ghetto. Thus, 'Pac sees himself as a particular case of the crucifixion of Black males in America. He willingly takes on the explicitly religious symbols associated with the Christ in order to stand in for all the "brothers" crucified by the media, presumably because the media refuses to understand the realities earlier discussed in this chapter. It is not enough, however, for Shakur alone to interpret his body in such symbolic terms. The religious reception of his bullet-riddled body by his community cements his symbolic status.

In "Followers of Black Jesus on Alert," Pinn and Easterling

depict the posthumous Tupac as a trickster figure who "slips between two worlds."[75] 'Pac presents himself as Christ on the *Makaveli* record, and after his death, there is a playfulness with respect to his return. What is important is not so much a literal resurrection and return. Rather, "Talk of Tupac's return, his continuing life, provides a critique of or signifies attempts to capture and control Black bodies…. This is the ability of said bodies to fight against restrictive forces. His invisibility for the moment is chosen not enforced, and it does not negate his significance, but rather intensifies it."[76] Such intensification is felt when hearing 'Pac's voice on his posthumously released albums (the first of which is *The Don Killuminati: The 7 Day Theory*). For the purposes of this chapter, I am less interested in the many speculations and theories regarding Tupac's actual death than the religious-symbolic interpretation of him/his body. Nas explicitly says of the slain rapper, "Tupac was Jesus Christ…He was a part of us."[77] Another fan says, "I worship 'Pac like Jesus Christ," precisely because 'Pac is despised like Christ was, and in so being symbolizes the perception of people of color in America.[78] Yet, how does this symbolism move one from being despised to simply being?

The religious symbolism of 2Pac's body is significant not simply because 'Pac's body carries the cries of a people, but also because in pointing to the grotesque, it fosters courage in the face of attacks upon the body and the psyche, including attacks from within one's self. On *The Don Killuminati: The 7 Day Theory*, Makaveli expresses the tension between self-hatred within the Black community and the resilience to keep moving in the face of

---

[75] Pinn and Easterling, "Followers of Black Jesus on Alert," 43.
[76] Ibid.
[77] Quoted in ibid., 42.
[78] Ibid.

all manner of trials. Such tension, it seems, is indicative of Shakur's own struggles with self-worth.[79] On "White Man'z World," Makaveli asks, "Why we act like we don't love ourselves?" He then urges African Americans, and women of color in particular, to be proud of being Black, of being the "have-nots." He goes on to dedicate the song to revolutionaries and political prisoners, including his godfather, the famous Black Panther Elmer "Geronimo" Pratt. In other tracks, 2Pac conveys resilience in the face of violence, as in "Life of an Outlaw," in which 'Pac describes himself as "scarred but still breathin'." Thus, there is a dialectic between doubt and self-hatred on the one hand, and pride and perseverance on the other. I suggest this dialectic ultimately reaches its resolution in what Paul Tillich calls the "courage to be."

"SCARRED BUT STILL BREATHING":

BLACK BODIES AND THE *COURAGE TO BE*

If we may place Tupac within Tillich's genealogy of philosophical and aesthetic articulations of the courage to be, he would likely fall in with the existentialist crowd, in which the courage to be is the courage to be *as oneself*. We have seen how Tupac expresses both "the anxiety of meaninglessness" and "the attempt to take this anxiety into the courage to be as oneself."[80] He courageously takes up the despair of his contexts (the penitentiary and the ghetto)—particularly their effects on the Black (male) body— as ultimate concern, like Kierkegaard and Kafka before him creatively expressing the meaninglessness daily encountered in the grotesque. James W. Perkinson explicitly draws parallels between 'Pac and Kierkegaard, saying, "Like [Kierkegaard] himself, Pac took up an existentialist focus upon the 'I' as moral imperative, pirouetted

---

[79] Dyson, *Holler If You Hear Me*, 241–42.
[80] Tillich, *The Courage to Be*, 139.

with panache across the life-scape of aesthetic and ethical and religious differentiation…and in an updated and postindustrial Socratic palaver, refused to seal any of the domains hermetically from the other."[81] Extending the similarities between the two thinker-artists, Perkinson notes that Shakur "danced 'macabre' in the theater of the inner city absurd, mourning his own losses of homies… careening close to being a killer in his lyric rages, and coveting his own demise at the end."[82] Makaveli waxes ironic—even and especially in his self-ironizing moments—as Perkinson's article title intimates, in order to "out the absurd." His courage to be as himself in the face of absurdity is what lends his body religious-symbolic significance, as others find in him courage to be as themselves as well.

While Tupac's dialectic of self-hatred and perseverance resolves itself in the courage to be as himself, listeners are left wondering whether Tupac personally and ultimately reaches the place of accepting his acceptance in spite of the perception of his unacceptableness.[83] Even so, his body (of work) remains symbolic of the need for the Black (male) body to be the subject of ultimate concern in the context of the many absurd realities surrounding police brutality and mass incarceration. So long as the bodies of Mike Brown, Eric Garner, Philando Castile, Terence Crutcher—as well as Black female bodies such as those of Sandra Bland and Rekia Boyd—and those of countless others continue to be lynched by agents of the state, the Makavelian crucifix cannot be traded for another symbol. The symbol of the ghetto's own Suffering Servant

---

[81] James W. Perkinson, "Illin' the Evil, Outing the Absurd: Kierke-gaardian Irony Meets Makavelian Grotesquery in the Postindustrial City," *Black Theology: An International Journal* 5/3 (2007): 373.

[82] Ibid.

[83] See Tillich, *The Courage to Be*, 164.

must remain in order to facilitate the courage of despair and, hopefully, the courage of self-affirmation.[84] With Dyson,[85] and in line with Tillich's assertion that symbols live and die,[86] one might hope for a day in which the stigmatized body of Tupac ceases to be a religious symbol because the absurdities called to account in such signification have ceased to exist. Until then, however, the wounds of the eternal thug continue to call attention to ghetto grotesquerie, and in so doing cultivate the courage to be even in the midst of despair and anxiety: "One love, one thug, one nation."

---

[84] Arguably, the contemporary work of Compton native Kendrick Lamar, who is in a sense a disciple of Tupac, gets closer to the courage of self-affirmation in a Tillichian sense. Note songs such as "Alright" and "i," on *To Pimp a Butterfly* (Santa Monica: Aftermath, Mar. 2015).

[85] Dyson, *Holler If You Hear Me*, xv–xxiv.

[86] Tillich, *Dynamics of Faith*, 49–50.

5

Disabled Bodies as Ultimate Concern

COURTNEY WILDER

Paul Tillich's account of Christ as the New Being includes both an analysis of sin as estrangement and an argument that Christ as Savior is a healer. These two aspects of Tillich's Christology exist in some tension with one another, and Tillich's exploration of Christ as a healer reinforces, rather than problematizes, stigmatizing accounts of disabled bodies within Christianity. Particularly troubling is Tillich's failure to disentangle the experience of disability from its associations with sin. However, while this characterization of Christ and of human beings is subject to fierce critique from theologians and sociologists of disability, Tillich himself provides the means of correction within his own systematic theology, namely the method of correlation. A close reading of Tillich, moreover, raises the possibility that he can be retrieved both as a theologian whose work is important to Christian reflection on disability, and possibly as a theologian with a disability. This suggests that Tillich's work, despite its flawed association of healing with salvation, may have important implications for a theology of disability and for exploring the existential significance of the human experience of disability.

CHRIST AS HEALER

First, a word about why theologians reflecting on disability reject what Nancy Eiesland has aptly and memorably called "sin-disability conflation."[1] The practice of implying or arguing outright that sin causes disability, and that having a disability reveals a person to be especially sinful, has long been embedded in Christian theology. Nor is this the only problematic Christian response to disability. The inverse claim, that disability is an indication or a cause of an elevated spiritual status, also fails to adequately address the situation of people living with disabilities. Eiesland writes,

> The biblical support of virtuous suffering has been a subtle, but particularly dangerous theology for persons with disabilities. Used to promote adjustment to unjust social situations and to sanction acceptance of isolation among persons with disabilities, it has encouraged our passivity and resignation and has institutionalized depression as an appropriate response to "divine testing." Viewing suffering as a means of purification and of gaining spiritual merit not only promotes the link between sin and disability but also implies that those who never experience a "cure" continue to harbor sin in their lives.[2]

Theologian Thomas Reynolds, building on Eiesland's critique of this conflation of sin and disability, writes,

> There are...unsound theological suppositions at work here. The linkage of sin-punishment-blemish with faith-forgiveness/salvation-healing claims too much....If it is taken for granted that God's power can and God's love wishes to

---

[1] Nancy Eiesland, *The Disabled God: Toward a Liberatory Theology of Disability* (Nashville: Abingdon Press, 1994) 72.
[2] Eiesland, *The Disabled God*, 73.

eliminate creaturely imperfection and suffering, restoring the dignity of health and wholeness, there must therefore be something that is blocking God's healing presence.[3]

Thus—as with Tillich's Christology—when Christ is identified as a healer, not only are people with disabilities seen as self-evidently in need of divine intervention, their faith is also questioned. They are doubly suspect: first there is whatever sinful action is presumed to have caused the disability in the first place, and second, God's apparent unwillingness to heal the disability is read as insufficient faith. Reynolds observes, "If God is not culpable, and a community refuses to question its social order and/or theological framework, then the individual is presumed at fault."[4] The effect of such doctrine is to reinforce stigma against people with disabilities and to increase isolation of people with disabilities from Christian religious communities.

Such an analysis also presumes a mistaken anthropology, wherein human beings are divided into binary categories: disabled and able-bodied. A more realistic account of human beings would reflect the fact that no person is exempt from the limits of human existence; Christ's purpose is not to selectively empower some people beyond their creaturely capacities. Theologian John Swinton, writing specifically about dementia, argues, "To be human is to be mortal, and mortality means that decay is inevitable. ...Our humanness is not diminished by dementia or any other condition. Such conditions are simply part of what it means to be human beings who are living out their lives in a creation which is broken but in the process of being redeemed."[5] As we will see, Tillich's theo-

---

[3] Thomas Reynolds, *Vulnerable Communion* (Grand Rapids: Brazos Press, 2008) 37.

[4] Reynolds, *Vulnerable Communion*, 37.

[5] John Swinton, *Dementia: Living in the Memories of God* (Grand Rap-

logical analysis of disability, particularly mental illness, is at odds with much theological reflection on disability.

EXPLICATING TILLICH

Contrary to the positions of Eiesland, Reynolds, and Swinton, Tillich strongly asserts that salvation entails being freed from impairment; that is, Tillich's account of Christ as healer reinforces the association of sin and disability and raises the possibility that Christian faith can provide restoration from disability. Tillich's position on healing and salvation appears most clearly in *Systematic Theology I*; in *Systematic Theology III*; in his sermons "On Healing I" and "On Healing II" in *The New Being*; and in his sermons "Heal the Sick; Cast Out the Demons" and "Salvation" in *The Eternal Now*. The sermon "Seeing and Hearing" in *The New Being* also offers a problematic analysis of the relationship of bodily impairment to the concept and experience of faith.

Theological reflections on disability and healing are not dominant themes in Tillich's thought but do recur as pervasive metaphors for describing the human relationship to Christ; healing and salvation are closely associated in Tillich's Christology. In the first volume of his *Systematic Theology*, Tillich writes, "Salvation is derived from *salvus*, 'healthy,' or 'whole,' and can be applied to every act of healing: to the healing of sickness, of demonic possession, and of servitude to sin and to the ultimate power of death. Salvation in this sense takes place in time and history, just as revelation takes place in time and history."[6] He reiterates the etymology and elaborates on this theme in his sermon "Salvation," writing, "Saving is healing from sickness and saving is delivering from servi-

---

ids: Eerdmans Publishing Company, 2012) 183–84.

  [6] Paul Tillich, *Systematic Theology*, 3 vols. (Chicago: University of Chicago Press, 1951–1963) 1:146.

tude; and the two are the same. ...We consider the neurotic or psychotic person who cannot face life as sick. ...He is, as the New Testament expresses it, demonically possessed."[7] According to Tillich's account, sickness, servitude, neurosis, psychosis, demon possession, and bondage to sin are all equally part of the human experience, and it is from these existential situations that Christ saves us.

In the third volume of the *Systematic Theology*, Tillich argues,

> It is now possible to relate the different ways of healing to the reality of the New Being and its significance for healing. ...At this point health and salvation are identical, both being the elevation of man to the transcendent unity of the divine life. The receiving function of man in this experience is faith; the actualizing function is love. Health in the ultimate sense of the word, health as identical with salvation, is life in faith and love.[8]

This pair of claims—that the receiving function of human beings in the experience of salvation is faith, and that health is salvation—suggests that faith is the experience not only of being healed, but of experiencing health *as restorative.*

Tillich mitigates his identification of salvation with healing in *Systematic Theology III* with the following caveat:

> The healing impact of the Spiritual Presence does not replace the ways of healing under the different dimensions of life.... [This] rejects not only the wrong claims of the faith healers but also the much more serious but rather popular error that derives disease directly from a particular sin or from a sinful life. Such an error produces a despairing conscience in those

---

[7] Paul Tillich, *The Eternal Now* (New York: Scribner, 1963) 114.
[8] Tillich, *Systematic Theology*, 3:280.

who are stricken and a pharisaic self-righteousness in those who are not. To be sure there is often a simple line of cause and effect between a sinful act or behavior and a particular incidence of disease. But even then, healing is not a matter of forgiveness alone but also a matter of medical or psychological care.[9]

Here Tillich roundly rejects faith healing in lieu of conventional medical care, but he affirms the connection between forgiveness and healing. His argument that sometimes behaviors that are considered "sinful" harm people is reasonable enough as an empirical observation, but the claim that people who have sinned, and whose behavior has caused them harm, need forgiveness in order to heal offers a strong justification for wrongly imputing sin to those who remain disabled. This is precisely the position that Reynolds argues against.

Thus, Tillich makes an ambiguous and complicated Christological claim: on the one hand, Christ is cast as a unifier of that which has become estranged, and Tillich rejects the "error" of blaming a person with a disability or chronic illness for his or her condition. On the other hand, Tillich is far from renouncing the connection between sin and disability so vigorously rejected by theologians of disability, including Eiesland, Reynolds, and Swinton. With the claim that healing is not a matter of forgiveness *alone,* Tillich reinforces the belief, prevalent in the Christian tradition and evident in the biblical texts, that bodily and psychological healing do to some degree require forgiveness of one's sins. This position strengthens rather than dismantles the very "pharisaic self-righteousness" of those who seek to make people with disabilities into objects of pity and charity, or make them into moral

---

[9] Ibid.

examples for the benefit of the able-bodied, or to exclude people with disabilities from the community of Christian practice.

Tillich's two sermons entitled "On Healing I" and "On Healing II" complicate matters further. The text for the first sermon is Matthew 10:1: "And he called to him his twelve disciples and gave them authority over unclean spirits, to cast them out, and to heal every disease and every infirmity." The text for the second sermon is a blend of Psalms 147 and 103: "The Lord healeth the broken in heart, and bideth up their wounds—Bless the Lord, O my soul…who healeth all thy diseases, who redeemeth thy life from destruction."[10]

Tillich opens the first sermon by describing a recent trip to Germany, where he encountered "a sick people, sick as a whole and sick as individuals."[11] The reason for this sickness, he says, is revealed in their "tales of horror, stories of pain and despair, anxieties dwelling in their blood."[12] The guilt he sees, the split in the nation, all speak to the sickness of the German people. At first he lauds those whom he encounters who have within themselves "a healing power, making them whole in spite of their disruption, making them serene in spite of their sorrow, making them examples for all of us, examples of what could and should happen to us!"[13] This is a striking contrast with his identification of Christ as the healer and his argument in *Systematic Theology III* that healing requires forgiveness; Tillich does not suggest here that salvation

---

[10] The individual sermons are undated but appear in a collected volume: Paul Tillich, *The New Being* (New York: Charles Scribner's Sons, 1955). The individual sermons in the volume are not dated.

[11] Ibid., 34. Despite that this story takes place after the end of World War II, this volume of sermons was published in 1955.

[12] Tillich, *The New Being*.

[13] Tillich, *The New Being*, 35. We might presume the "us" refers to his American audience.

from God is what has provided this experience of healing.

Next, Tillich goes on to describe the deceptively healthy-seeming Americans whom one encounters in everyday life. The difference between the Americans and the Germans, he argues, is that the former hide their sickness. Despite Americans' apparent capacity to engage in self-reflection on social issues like "discrimination, exploitation, destructive competition," and their political freedom, Tillich argues that data on high rates of mental illness among prospective participants in the U.S. military tell another story, one that suggests a deep-seated existential problem.[14] This claim is in some tension with Tillich's observation in "Heal the Sick; Cast Out the Demons" (discussed below) that a society itself may need healing in the form of liberation. In "On Healing I," American response to social injustice does not seem to Tillich to warrant an understanding of American culture as healthy.

He continues by comparing the genuinely healthy German people to the unhealthy Americans he sees at home:

> [M]any in our nation [that is, the U.S.] cannot stand this health. They want sickness as a refuge into which they can escape from the harshness of an insecure life. And since the medical care has made it more difficult to escape into bodily illness, they choose *mental* illness. …[W]e dislike our sickness with some parts of our souls; but we like it with some other parts, mostly unconsciously, sometimes even consciously.[15]

Here, Tillich argues that because effective medical treatment for many health problems is available, it may be difficult to attain physical illness through the force of one's will. However, he ar-

---

14 Tillich, *The New Being*, 35.
15 Tillich, *The New Being*, 36.

gues, mental illness is less easily treated and thus an appealing ave-
nue for those who might want to become ill to "exercise power
through weakness."[16] This implies that in earlier periods, where
medical care was less adequate, people chose physical illness as a
means of escaping life. This argument is uncomfortably discordant
with modern diagnostic practices; many physicians today recognize that both physical and mental illnesses have genetic, social,
and environmental causes, some of which are still poorly understood. Tillich's understanding of the etiology of mental illness, in
particular, is now outdated and overly simplified. Lest his listeners
miss the connection between intentionally cultivated mental illness
and sin, he warns: "Don't underestimate this temptation."[17]

Tillich's shorthand explication of Paul in this sermon—
specifically, the depiction of people exercising power through
weakness—bears some analysis. He is pointing the listener to 2
Corinthians 12:7–9. Paul writes,

> Therefore, to keep me from being too elated, a thorn was
> given to me in the flesh, a messenger of Satan to torment me,
> to keep me from being too elated.[8] Three times I appealed to
> the Lord about this, that it would leave me,[9] but he said to
> me, "My grace is sufficient for you, for power is made perfect
> in weakness." So, I will boast all the more gladly of my
> weaknesses, so that the power of Christ may dwell in me.

What about Paul's description of this thorn could lead Tillich's listener or reader, or any Christian, into temptation? Tillich
is making two claims here: One, people choose mental illness vol-
untarily as a sort of self-cancellation strategy because they are una-
ble or unwilling to cope with the requirements of everyday life,

---

[16] Tillich, *The New Being*, 36.
[17] Tillich, *The New Being*, 36.

wrongly believing that this will provide them with power. Two, despite the apparent biblical warrant for reading illness as a perfection of power, this choice is not only a mistake, but a temptation, that is, it is sinful. Tillich is arguing that only a serious misreading of Paul could support such an action, and that it is a serious error to mistake mental illness for something powerful. Indeed, given that Paul specifically recounts having begged God to remove this thorn—whatever it was—Tillich seems to be warning his listener against a misreading that would be virtually impossible to support biblically. However, using this rejection of an unlikely misreading as a rhetorical strategy, Tillich suggests that power can only properly be exercised through health. This reification of psychological health, as we will see below, leads Tillich down a problematic path.

Instead of illness being mistaken for power, he argues, salvation should be associated with wholeness and health. Explicating the social situation of the gospels, so as to set up his depiction of Christ as Healer, Tillich explores the social analysis of illness offered by the Greeks and Jews of Jesus' period: "They called the mentally ill the possessed or demoniacs and they tried to expel the evil spirits. They also knew that nations can be sick and that the diseases of social classes infect every individual in it."[18] This is an allusion to the pericope of the Gerasene demoniac; Mark 5:9–10 (parallel: Luke 8) provides this exchange between Jesus and the demons occupying a man who is unclean, possessed, and lives among the tombs. The man is often captured and chained up by locals, but has great physical strength, allowing him to escape containment: "Then Jesus asked him, 'What is your name?' He replied, 'My name is Legion; for we are many.'[10] He begged him

---

[18] Tillich, *The New Being*, 37.

earnestly not to send them out of the country." On Tillich's reading, here not only is the body of the individual man contaminated by these demons, but the man's illness is reflective of the illness of the whole nation; political occupation, then, is represented by demon possession (hence the name "Legion") and is analogous to mental illness. In Tillich's view, Jesus emerges in response to the tremendous need for "health and wholeness." He writes, "Salvation and a savior were expected. But salvation is healing. And the savior is the healer."[19] Bodily healing of an individual with mental illness and restoration of health to the whole nation can both be attributed to Jesus and discerned in this one narrative about the Gerasene man. This Christology stands over and against the practice that Tillich identifies among Americans of cultivating illness to escape from reality and attempt to garner power. Unfortunately, Tillich's reading of the biblical passage reinforces the stigmatizing of people living with mental illness as deliberately and sinfully choosing those illnesses.

Tillich insists that such healing was not one miraculous indicator of many that demonstrated Jesus' identity, but that Jesus' healing practices were central to his incarnation: "Jesus answers the anxious questions of the Baptist about whether He is the Savior, by pointing to His healing power. This is what He says: 'If I am able to heal the deaf and blind, if I am able to liberate the mentally sick, then a new reality has come upon you!'"[20] Tillich emphasizes that the healing stories of the gospels are not simply historical narratives, but "healing stories of the present. …They show the human situation, the relation between bodily and mental disease, between sickness and guilt, between the desire of being healed and

---

[19] Tillich, *The New Being*, 37.
[20] Tillich, *The New Being*, 37.

the fear of being healed."[21] Key to the expression of Jesus' power as Savior, then, is human willingness to confront guilt and be healed.

In "On Healing II," Tillich continues in the same vein. He argues, "...the demoniac who met [Jesus] was liberated from his mental cleavage. Those who are disrupted, split, disintegrated, are healed by Him." This, Tillich says, is the meaning of the Kingdom of God. He quotes Matthew 10:7–8a: "As ye go, preach, saying, the Kingdom of God is at hand. Heal the sick, raise the dead, cleanse the lepers, cast out demons." Tillich writes, "That is what they shall do and for *this* He gives them authority and power; for in Him the kingdom of God has appeared, and its nature is salvation, healing that which is ill, making whole what is broken."[22] Salvation can be initiated by Jesus' followers insofar as they engage in this task of reunification and healing.

The language of this sermon is especially problematic in that Tillich is actively taking to task theologians and pastors for their failure to depict the power of Jesus as healer. He writes, "...[W]e are responsible, ministers, laymen, theologians, who forgot that 'Savior' means 'healer,' he who makes whole and sane what is broken and insane, in body and mind. The woman who encountered Him was made whole, the demoniac who met him was liberated from his mental cleavage. Those who are disrupted, split, disintegrated, are healed by Him."[23] Remarkably, given his sophisticated analysis of symbols in *Dynamics of Faith*, Tillich engages in very little discussion in this sermon of interpreting miracles symbolically. Indeed, the first paragraph of the sermon is dismissive of attempts to "paint" Jesus in sermons as a "moral teacher...social re-

---

[21] Tillich, *The New Being*, 36.
[22] Tillich, *The New Being*, 44.
[23] Tillich, *The New Being*, 43.

former…[or] suffering servant."[24] He writes later on, "Of course, we were and we are worried about the abuse of religious healing for commercial and other selfish purposes or about its distortion into magic and superstition. But abuses occur when the right use is lacking and superstitions arise when faith has become weak."[25] Finally, he exhorts his listeners to engage in self-reflection: "Are we healed, have we received healing forces…? Are we grasped by this power? Is it strong enough to overcome our neurotic trends, the rebellion of unconscious strivings, the spilt in our conscious being, the diseases which disintegrate our minds and destroy our bodies at the same time?"[26] Here Tillich rejects commonplace symbolic interpretations of Jesus' healing, warns against faith healing, and then argues that the pastor or theologian himself or herself needs to have experienced healing to properly understand and proclaim the gospel. He identifies this as "the real problem."[27] This strongly suggests that bodily and psychological wholeness reflects a proper having-been-grasped by the healing power of Christ; the corollary implication is that remaining experiences of disability are evidence that one has not really encountered Christ.

Two sermons in *The Eternal Now* also focus on biblical texts about healing. The first is "Heal the Sick; Cast Out the Demons," a 1955 commencement address delivered at Union Theological Seminary in New York.[28] The second is entitled "Salvation." In "Heal the Sick," Tillich again takes up Matthew 10:8. Tillich frames the sermon for the occasion, telling the graduating students, many of whom are about to enter into professional ministry,

---

[24] Tillich, *The New Being*, 43.
[25] Tillich, *The New Being*, 43.
[26] Tillich, *The New Being*, 43.
[27] Tillich, *The New Being*, 44.
[28] Tillich, *The Eternal Now*, 58.

that the first difficulty they will encounter is that "many people will tell you that they do not need to be healed."[29] He first qualifies the biblical instruction, reminding the students that healing is not confined to the church, and that a pastor has no "special prerogative" to heal.[30] Next, he cautions them against expecting to perform outright faith healings, saying, "It is an abuse of the name of Christ to use it as a magic formula."[31] Neither, Tillich warns, can students simply skirt issues of theodicy when engaging in healing. It is natural for people to wonder why sickness is "part of the divine order of things" if it exists only to be healed.[32] The newly graduated pastors, Tillich says, should not attempt to set this question aside by chalking the purpose of sickness up to the mysterious ways of God. "Of course there is mystery—divine mystery—and in contrast to it, the mystery of evil....Evil in the divine order is not only a mystery; it is also a revelation. ...He who can become sick is greater than he who cannot."[33] Tillich has neatly entered into the first and the second pitfall Eiesland identifies, simultaneously ascribing illness to demonic influences and suggesting that those who can become ill have a spiritual privilege of some kind over and against those who cannot. Somewhat paradoxically, even those favored ones who can become sick need healing: "Healing is the act of reuniting [divergent trends in our bodily or mental or spiritual life] after the disruption of their unity."[34] Tillich identifies the sick, then, as susceptible to demons, and also more capable of receiving revelation, and also in need of healing attention from the newly-minted pastors who are hearing the ser-

---

[29] Tillich, *The Eternal Now*, 58.
[30] Tillich, *The Eternal Now*, 59.
[31] Tillich, *The Eternal Now*, 60.
[32] Tillich, *The Eternal Now*, 60.
[33] Tillich, *The Eternal Now*, 61.
[34] Tillich, *The Eternal Now*, 61.

mon.

Then Tillich's sermon takes a turn that is somewhat more promising in terms of his analysis of disability; he offers a critique of the social practice of distancing oneself or one's group from those who are regarded as contaminants: "It may well be that the disease of many churches, denominations, and congregations is that they try to escape disease by cutting off what can produce disease, and also what can produce greatness of life."[35] Tillich reminds his listeners that grace is the healing power that God provides, and then says, "You have learned that disease that seems bodily may be mental at root, and that a disease that seems individual may be social at the same time, and that you cannot heal individuals without liberating them from the social demons that have contributed to their sickness."[36] This is remarkably similar to Eiesland's sociologically-framed argument about the experience of people with disabilities. She writes, "People with disabilities have been encouraged to see our needs as unique and extraordinary, rather than as society-wide issues of inclusion and exclusion."[37] Eiesland suggests instead that it is *society* that needs healing and transformation, rather than the bodies of individual people with disabilities. Similarly, Tillich's language has shifted from a focus on bodily healing to social liberation, suggesting that the bodies of the "sick" are not the only, and perhaps not the primary, issue that pastors need to address when ministering to and seeking to heal within their congregations. This is not the central focus of the sermon and does not mitigate the association of disability, sin, and demonic possession, but this shift points toward a possible Tillichian tact for Christian reflection on disability.

---

[35] Tillich, *The Eternal Now*, 62.
[36] Tillich, *The Eternal Now*, 63.
[37] Eiesland, *The Disabled God*, 28.

The sermon entitled "Salvation" in *The Eternal Now* serves to elaborate upon the Christology Tillich proposes in *Systematic Theology I*: Christ as Healer. Tillich takes as his text Matthew 6:13b: "Save us from the evil one." Having discussed the origin of the term "savior," he writes, "Salvation happens whenever the enslaving power is conquered, whenever the wall is broken through, whenever the sickness is healed. He who can do this is called the savior. Nobody except God can do this."[38] Tillich observes that the term "salvation" and related words must be used in preaching: "It is necessary...for the words which are most used in religion are also those whose genuine meaning is almost completely lost and whose impact on the human mind is nearly negligible. Such words must be reborn, if possible, and thrown away if this is not possible."[39] This claim reveals both Tillich's deep commitment to taking religious language seriously (his frequent use of "estrangement" as a replacement for "sin," for example) and also his failure to consider the possibility that metaphors of disability might serve his purposes badly and actually cause harm. As with his other sermons and the *Systematic Theology*, while Tillich's use of "sickness" to explore the reality of sin and the experience of salvation is in some sense metaphorical, he consistently reinforces rather than problematizes the long-held association of sin and illness. The proposed rebirth of religious language does not extend very far.

As the sermon continues, Tillich reflects on the healing narratives in the Bible. He writes, "There are three types [of healing stories]: those in which people sick of body are directly healed; those in which people sick of body are forgiven and healed; and those in which people sick of mind are delivered from what was

---

[38] Tillich, *The Eternal Now*, 115.
[39] Tillich, *The Eternal Now*, 113.

called demonic possession."[40] Typical of his biblical hermeneutic, Tillich rejects a literal reading of the healing stories: "It is regrettable that most preaching emphasizes the miraculous character of these stories, often using a poor, superstitious notion of miracles instead of showing the profound insight they betray into disease, health, and healing—the inseparable unity of body and mind."[41] Tillich regards the misreading of these narratives as regrettable, as it prevented the church from properly understanding the experience of healing from physical or mental illness. "If we look at the miracles of medical and mental healing today, we must say that here the wall between eternal and perishable life is pierced at *one* point; that liberation from the evil one has happened in *one* dimension of our life; that a physician or mental helper becomes a savior for someone."[42] While Tillich's analysis does evoke a powerful experience, he ignores the other implications of this reading of healing texts: the suggestion that those who do not seem to have been adequately healed do not have faith or that God does not love them; the presumption that an impaired body is an unsaved or unsaveable body; the implication that all people with disabilities are in fact seeking bodily or psychological healing; the suggestion that recovery from illness is perhaps the only way to properly understand divine salvation.

Tillich warns that there are two possible limits to this understanding of healing and salvation. One, healing does not provide immortality or invincibility: "The people who were healed by Jesus became sick again and died. Those who were liberated from demonic compulsion might, as Jesus himself warned, relapse into

---

[40] Tillich, *The Eternal Now*, 116.
[41] Tillich, *The Eternal Now*, 116.
[42] Tillich, *The Eternal Now*, 117.

more serious states of mental disease."[43] This is certainly a pragmatic observation, but Tillich fails to consider that perhaps if bodily or psychological healing is limited and temporary it is not the best opportunity for human beings to seek understanding of salvation. He continues, describing the second limit to the analysis: "The attitude of him who is to be healed may prevent healing. Without the desire for delivery from the evil one there is no liberation; without longing for healing power, no healing!"[44] This claim is parallel to the set of observations Tillich makes in "On Healing I" regarding the seemingly-healthy Americans who actually choose illness in the mistaken belief that it will bring them power. While Christian teachings regarding the individual agency of a person in effecting his or her salvation differ widely, Tillich seems to be using a particular construct of the individual's relationship with God as his template and reverse-engineering a rather faulty analysis of illness here. The metaphor once again fails to hold, particularly in the absence of a medical perspective that finds people responsible for their own illnesses. Furthermore, Tillich again constructs a reading of disabled bodies as sinful bodies. If his position (that a person must desire healing in order to be healed) is taken to its logical conclusion, then lack of healing reveals also lack of desire to be well.

Throughout his sermons, Tillich consistently aligns bodily and mental health with faith and salvation; he associates impairment and illness with sin, estrangement, and political oppression. While mental illness is the primary focus of Tillich's theology of healing in the sermons, he also uses the ability to see as a metaphor for faithfulness. For example, in his sermon "Seeing and Hearing," on John 9:39–41, the tail end of the pericope that de-

---

[43] Tillich, *The Eternal Now*, 117.
[44] Tillich, *The Eternal Now*, 117.

scribes the healing of the man born blind, he argues, "That which we have seen with our eyes according to the gospel is the Word, the eternal Word or Logos in whom God speaks, who can be seen through the works of creation and who is visible in the man Jesus. The Word can be *seen*, this is the highest unity of hearing and seeing."[45] Thus, in Tillich's repetition of the biblical metaphor, the encounter with God incarnate is dependent on the capacity to see. He continues, "Our Gospel calls us blind, all of us. And Jesus says that we are blind because we believe we see and do not know that we are blind; and He threatens that we shall be thrown into more blindness if we insist that we are seeing."[46] Although Tillich goes on in the sermon to describe the drawbacks to trying to see God— one might become drawn in by "idols, fascinating, horrible, overwhelming in seductive beauty or destructive power"—the problem is again described metaphorically as the lack of capacity to see properly.[47] Faith equals sight just as salvation equals healing.

PROBLEMS OF TILLICH'S APPROACH:
IDOLATRY AND ESTRANGEMENT

One significant problem with Tillich's analysis of faith and healing is that he reifies the whole and healthy body at the expense of the disabled, estranged body. If, as he suggests, salvation is a restoration of health and unity to the body and psyche, the whole, intact body is idealized to the degree that it can be idolized. To critique Tillich properly on this point, we need only to return to his description of idolatry, in his sermon "Seeing and Hearing" and in *Dynamics of Faith*. The language of the sermon is gripping; Tillich warns us against "idols, fascinating, horrible, overwhelming

---

[45] Tillich, *The New Being*, 127.
[46] Tillich, *The New Being*, 131.
[47] Tillich, *The New Being*, 132.

in seductive beauty or destructive power." But images of God are not the only idols. As Tillich writes in *Dynamics of Faith*, "...everything which is a matter of unconditional concern is made into a god. If the nation is someone's ultimate concern, the name of the nation becomes a sacred name and the nation receives divine qualities which far surpass the reality of the being and functioning of the nation. The nation, then, stands in for and symbolizes the true ultimate, but in an idolatrous way."[48] Similarly, if the able-bodied person, and the healing and wholeness that he or she represents to Tillich, becomes his symbol of faith and reconciliation with the divine, then what Reynolds calls the "cult of normalcy" becomes idolatrous.

Reynolds argues, "Too often theology simply presumes the operative sway of the cult of normalcy, and in a way that is oppressive for persons with disabilities."[49] He identifies a phenomenon he calls "body capital" wherein bodies that are "marked by incompleteness or incompetence in form and/or function," bodies that lack capacity and thus capital, are marginalized.[50] Compare this with Tillich's critique of Americans with mental illness: "They want sickness as a refuge into which they can escape from the harshness of an insecure life. And since the medical care has made it more difficult to escape into bodily illness, they choose *mental illness*."[51] The loss of body capital is glossed as intentional escape, and Tillich argues that a person with mental illness is ill by choice. Critiqued as sinful, he or she is thereby both marginalized and also blamed for the circumstances of the marginalization.

---

[48] Paul Tillich, *Dynamics of Faith* (New York: Harper-Collins, 1957) 44.

[49] Reynolds, *Vulnerable Communion*, 28.

[50] Reynolds, *Vulnerable Communion*, 59.

[51] Tillich, *The New Being*, 36.

This particular idealization of healthy bodies, coming on the heels of Nazi practices of targeting people with disabilities for execution, is remarkably problematic, especially for as ardent an opponent of the Nazis as Tillich. Tillich's removal from his teaching position by the Nazis in April 1933, followed by his immigration to the United States at the invitation of Reinhold Niebuhr, and his vocal opposition to the Nazi government throughout the war, are well documented.[52] Nor was he unmoved by Nazi atrocities. His biographers Wilhelm and Marion Pauck describe him as having been sent into "an emotional tailspin" by news of Nazi brutalities emerging in late 1939.[53] Members of Tillich's own family, his sister and her husband and daughter, survived the war, and Tillich visited Germany shortly after the war ended.[54] So he certainly did not lack access to information regarding the Nazi regime's viciousness, including its treatment of people with intellectual, physical, and psychological disabilities.

Beginning in 1933, people with a wide range of disabilities were subject to compulsory sterilization in Germany.[55] Wards were established throughout Germany beginning in 1940 for the express purpose of executing children with disabilities.[56] Adults with disabilities were also euthanized; this met with some protest on the part of religious authorities.[57] Somewhere around 750,000 people with disabilities were executed by the Nazis, and this work

---

[52] See Wilhelm Pauck and Marion Pauck, *Paul Tillich, His Life & Thought* (New York: Harper & Row, 1976) ch. 5 and 6.

[53] Pauck and Pauck, *Paul Tillich*, 197.

[54] Pauck and Pauck, *Paul Tillich*, 197 .

[55] Suzanne Evans, *Forgotten Crimes: The Holocaust and People with Disabilities* (Chicago: Ivan R. Dee, 2004) 18.

[56] Evans, *Forgotten Crimes*, 26.

[57] Evans, *Forgotten Crimes*, 48.

was actively celebrated by the participants in these killings.[58] The selection of people with disabilities for genocide was not an incidental feature of Nazi ideology, but a key component of the larger program of eugenics. What Tillich's unreflective use of the healed, whole body as a metaphor for salvation does, then, is to perpetuate a particularly horrifying and vicious use of bodily imagery, where the healthy body is symbolic of moral goodness. Tillich does not offer any critique of what Reynolds calls the "cult of normalcy" and this failure is a serious problem for his Christology.[59]

What impact might this have? Consider Tillich's willingness to unreflectively use the metaphor of blindness to speak about lack of faith. Again he perpetuates, rather than confronts, the problem of estrangement as it is manifest in marginalization of people with disabilities. Theologian Amos Yong observes,

> In the ancient world, the disability metaphors communicated successfully to non-disabled people only because of the presumed correlation that existed between outward forms and inward realities....[B]lindness as a spiritual condition only makes sense because literal blindness refers to the incapacity to see and understand things clearly and make one's way about the world.[60]

Tillich relies on this metaphor from the biblical text but does not recognize it as an example of estrangement. The familiar imagery of the man who is blind and then sees confuses the condition

---

[58] Evans, *Forgotten Crimes*, 18, 64–65.

[59] This problem does not disappear once we take a closer look at Tillich's own history of mental illness (if anything, it becomes more serious). The power of anti-disability eugenics propaganda in both Germany and the U.S. in the 1930s and 1940s may have played a role in Tillich's oversight here, however.

[60] Amos Yong. *The Bible, Disability, and the Church* (Grand Rapids: Eerdmans) 26.

of bodily impairment with the experience of spiritual impairment and estrangement from others, from oneself, and from God. While this is a common enough interpretation of the text, its popularity does not make it less problematic to people with disabilities, who are once again cast as exemplars of the unfaithful.

Tillich's interpretation and proclamation tread the same ground as those who would adhere to and reinforce a social situation we can rightly name as sinful: the stigmatization, even unto death, of people with disabilities, whether physical or intellectual or psychological, and the exclusion of people with disabilities from the goods in which all other members of society are invited to share.

This is all the more intriguing because of Tillich's own experience of psychological unrest, and the otherwise fruitful possibility of the method of correlation for disability theology. Tillich provides a theological method, but does not employ it to investigate the existential situation of disability as an experience of sin—not sin as he construes it, choosing disability to avoid life, not sin which is punished by God by means of bodily impairment, but sin as the estrangement of a person living with a disability from his or her family, society, and religious community. In short, Tillich misses the estrangement and employs metaphorical language to describe faith that instead points us toward idolatry. He also seems, perhaps unconsciously, to identify people who are in some important ways much like himself as particularly prone to temptation and sin.

RETRIEVAL OF TILLICH'S SOTERIOLOGY

What can be done to retrieve Tillich's thinking here? How can the experience of disability be understood as religiously significant using the method of correlation? To what extent is Tillich a theologian of and/or with a disability? How can his critique of idolatry serve to dismantle the estrangement between people with and without disability? The method of correlation provides us with the means to correct Tillich's analysis of disability and to reject his reiteration of metaphors that further marginalize people with disabilities.

Tillich argues,

> Systematic theology uses the method of correlation. It has always done so, sometimes more, sometimes less, consciously, and must do so consciously and outspokenly, especially if the apologetic point of view is to prevail. The method of correlation explains the contents of the Christian faith through existential questions and theological answers in mutual interdependence.[62]

Some of those existential questions have to do with the human experience of disability. In order to fully understand and articulate the questions posed by human existence, Tillich argues, we must use disciplines other than theology, including philosophy, various branches of the sciences, history, psychology, and sociology.[63] Thus, no exploration of the religious significance of disability, no investigation of those existential questions, will be complete without disability theory, without sociology and history. These are exactly the disciplines that provide the basis for critique of Christian response to disability and that inform theologians of disability. Tillich's description of the method of correlation includes the built-in corrective of responding to disciplines outside theology when articulating the theological answers to existential questions.

At this point we ought to consider Tillich's own situation. He

---

[62] Tillich, *Systematic Theology*, 1:60.
[63] Tillich, *Systematic Theology*, 1:18.

writes in *Systematic Theology I,*

> Only those who have experienced the shock of transitoriness, the anxiety in which they are aware of their finitude, the threat of non-being, can understand what the notion of God means. Only those who have experienced the tragic ambiguities of our historical existence and have totally questioned the meaning of existence can understand what the symbol of the Kingdom of God means.[64]

As Terry Cooper argues in his book *Paul Tillich and Psychology,*

> Tillich was not simply a brilliant abstract thinker who remained detached from the "up close and personal" dimensions of human agony. In fact, Tillich's experience, especially in World War I, seems to reaffirm Luther's rather famous comment that "a theologian is born by living, nay by dying and being damned, not by thinking, reading, and speculating."[65]

Cooper details Tillich's military service during the First World War. Tillich served as a chaplain and soldier from 1914–1919. "Tillich watched many friends and excellent soldiers die. He literally dug grave after grave as he buried friends, many of them disfigured, without caskets."[66] Cooper also describes Tillich's lifelong experience of anxiety: "On three occasions, Tillich experienced acute traumatic stress disorder which hospitalized him. While he regained his stamina fairly quickly, these acute reactions led to an untreated posttraumatic stress disorder, a condition with which he

---

[64] Tillich, *Systematic Theology,* 1:62.

[65] Terry D. Cooper, *Paul Tillich and Psychology: Historic and Contemporary Explorations in Theology, Psychotherapy, and Ethics,* Mercer Tillich Studies (Macon: Mercer University Press, 2006) 38.

[66] Cooper, *Paul Tillich and Psychology,* 40.

probably struggled the rest of his life."[67]

Pauck and Pauck describe Tillich's war years similarly: "For Tillich, it remained to visit the wounded, comfort the dying, and bury the fallen. His emotional and mental anguish was beyond words."[68] He was tested psychologically and theologically by his experiences. In 1918, he wrote to his father asking for help securing a job in Berlin, away from the front: "Body and soul are broken and can never be entirely repaired, but that is a small sacrifice in comparison with millions who have given their lives."[69] This damage, Pauck and Pauck argue, was "permanent and beyond repair," and influenced Tillich's sense of himself as a theologian of the boundary: split by his experiences.[70]

It seems possible that Tillich is under-recognized as a person with a disability—that is, a mental illness caused by trauma—and thus as a theologian with a disability. As he argues in *Systematic Theology I*, this experience provided him with powerful, theologically robust existential experiences—the shock of transitoriness, the threat of non-being—that form the basis of his account of the human relationship to God. Consider a passage from his sermon "On Healing": "Have we overcome in moments of grace the torturing anxiety in the depth of our hearts, the restlessness which never ceases moving and whipping us, the unordered desires and the hidden repressions which return as poisonous hate, the hostility against ourselves and others, against life itself, the hidden will to death?"[71] This description of anguish is vivid and personal. While Tillich does not explicitly lay out the connections between his ser-

---

[67] Cooper, *Paul Tillich and Psychology*, 41.
[68] Pauck and Pauck, *Paul Tillich*, 49.
[69] Ibid., 45.
[70] Ibid., 59.
[71] Tillich, *The New Being*, 45.

vice during the war and his experiences of anxiety in this sermon, he seems to be engaged in existential reflection of a very personal kind here.

Cooper argues that Tillich's daughter, Dr. Mutie Tillich Farris, read about "some key symptoms of posttraumatic stress disorder" and was "certain" that Tillich suffered from this disorder.[72] Retroactive diagnosis of any particular mental illness, and the argument that such an illness constitutes a disability, can only be done speculatively, and cannot be done on the basis of a few lines from a sermon.[73] But Tillich's association of what he calls "the anxiety in which [one is] aware of [his or her] finitude" with theological insight suggests that there are fruitful possibilities for a Tillichian theology of disability underlying his association of disability with intentional illness, estrangement, and lack of faith. Certainly, he seems deeply familiar with the experience of anxiety and despair; he also seems to argue that it can be the source of important theological insights. That is, he suggests that a person struggling with anxiety might be positioned to be a better theologian than he or she would otherwise be. What this provides for modern readers of Tillich is a means of engaging with Tillich as a theologian of disability, who characterizes anxiety as a powerful existential experience. Rather than a sharp divide between Tillich and those with illness whose experiences he associates with sin, we see at most a very fine line between Tillich and the people with illness he describes.[74]

---

[72] Cooper, *Paul Tillich and Psychology*, 41.

[73] In addition, diagnosis of anyone's mental illness should be done only by a qualified psychologist or psychiatrist, which I am not. The issue of what, precisely, constitutes a disability is also complicated, so whether the term applies to Tillich or not remains somewhat unclear.

[74] Any development of this position ought to be done with careful consideration of Nancy Eiesland's warning—invoked at the beginning of this

Need Tillich's Christology, which characterizes Christ as healer, be wholly overhauled? Is his reliance on healing as a symbol still potentially meaningful for Christians concerned with issues of disability? What new light might Tillich's own psychological history shed upon the problem of his analysis of illness? Tillich's concepts of Christ as Healer and sin as estrangement, despite their many problems, may still have great promise for a theology of disability. The key is to use Tillich's own method of correlation, and his own critique of idolatry, in reinterpreting the symbol of Christ as Healer. Many theologians of disability argue that disabled bodies should not be stigmatized as sinful and that people with disabilities can and should be valued members of Christian communities. Tillich's analysis of sin, and the symbol of Christ as Healer, must be properly oriented: the sin is to be found in the stigmatizing and marginalizing of people with disabilities, not in disabled bodies. If the idealized, idolized "perfect" body can be recognized as a sinful illusion and rejected as a religious norm, then the symbol of Christ as Healer can be retrieved.

Christ as the Healer of our estranged communities, rather than Christ who heals bodies or minds, is a salvific figure for people with and without disabilities. Christ who restores us to and with love, rather than Christ who makes the blind see, is a salvific Christ. Retrieved as a theologian with and of disability, Tillich provides us with a method to more fully understand and reflect upon the experience of disability. He holds that anxiety and recognition of one's finitude warrant existential analysis. As Swinton argues, this is not sin to be erased but central to our very humanness: "Such conditions are simply part of what it means to be human beings who are living out their lives in a creation which is

---

chapter—against "[v]iewing suffering as a means of purification and of gaining spiritual merit" (Eiesland, *The Disabled God*, 73).

broken but in the process of being redeemed."[75] Tillich argues in his sermon "To Whom Much Is Forgiven…": "We feel rejected by life, not so much because of its objective darkness and threats and horrors, but because of our estrangement from its power and meaning. He who is reunited with God, the creative Ground of life, the power of life in everything that lives, is reunited with life. …He understands that the greater the love is, the greater the estrangement which is conquered by it."[76] The implied promise of this vision of healing is a human community devoted to identifying the sinful barriers that separate its members from one another and from God, and eradicating them. From taking pragmatic steps to address architectural barriers and other accessibility issues to recognizing the spiritual harm that is done to those whose bodies are denigrated and marginalized, the work of Christ as Healer can liberate all people.

---

[75] Swinton, *Dementia*, 183–84.
[76] Tillich, *The New Being*, 11.

6

Cyborgs and the Techno-Monstrous Body

ADAM PRYOR

Various forms of postmodernist discourse giving prominence to identity and experience as sources of theology reveal that bodies are slippery. The conceptualization is slippery because bodies resist being neatly tied to static, essentialist notions of selfhood. Bodies are distinctive in their performances (to borrow Judith Butler's term) and bear the marks and scars of their particular performances from which dynamic notions of selfhood might arise. As a source for theological reflection, we can no longer make recourse to *the* body as a static foundation upon which various senses of self can be built; instead, we must carefully consider how *each* body, *any* body, performs so as to better appreciate how the plurality and distinctiveness of bodily variety affect a sense of "selfhood."

The existential analytic of Paul Tillich's theology holds a curious place in this stream of thinking. His notion of "self" is far more dynamic than typical static, essentialist accounts stemming from an enlightenment heritage. However, any serious wrestling with our understanding of body will have an impact on the structural conditions of Tillich's theological efforts, because the body dwells at the border between self and world that grounds Tillich's ontological reflections. As such, the body is a serious problem for constructive theological work done in a Tillichian vein. Our initial impulse may be simply to assert that reflecting on the body provides a particular mechanism for revealing foundational issues of ultimacy. In such a case, any particular body could be the exemplar from which we understand underlying questions of *the* body (an abstracted, universalized body) in order to present a series of existential questions that we can easily subvert into his method of correlation. Yet, does such an understanding really give sufficient attention to the distinctiveness of each body's performativity and its particularity? I think not.

In his short work *Love, Power, and Justice*, Tillich identifies four principles of justice that can be indexical criteria in identifying how particular concerns might legitimately claim ultimacy. This chapter will analyze Tillich's account of these four principles of justice (adequacy, equality, personality, and liberty) and suggest that a proper symbol of ultimate concern should be one that seeks unity between self and world while promoting a sense of justice.

Drawing on this analysis, I will consider the place of technologically enhanced bodies, cyborgs, as a means of realizing ultimate concern. In offering this account of cyborg bodies, I will give special attention to discourse concerning post-humanism (especially in light of critiques offered by disability theology) and the monstrous stranger. In both discourses, understanding the social location, in terms of dystopic despair or utopic hope, crucially shapes the way in which the technologically enhanced body can serve as a realization of ultimate concern.

ULTIMATE CONCERN, JUSTICE, AND
THE ISSUE OF FINAL REVELATION

In his *Systematic Theology*, Tillich begins his discussion of the meaning of God through a phenomenological description: God is humankind's ultimate concern—the answering correlate to the implied question of our finite being. There is, though, a tension between what is "ultimate" and what is "of concern" that Tillich identifies as "an inescapable inner tension in the idea of God."[1] The index of our concern, our ability to be concerned, is in direct correlation to the concreteness of the object of our concern. For a universal concept to be of concern at all requires its representation through finite, concrete experiences. In contrast, for something to be truly ultimate, it must transcend everything finite and concrete. As this transcendence occurs, though, the ultimate becomes increasingly abstract. This is the inner tension of our being ultimately concerned.

Tillich applies this tension of ultimate concern to the doctrine of God. If God is what concerns humankind ultimately, then as God is identified with and through finite, concrete experiences, our concern is increasingly engaged—God becomes ever more recognizably present—but at the expense of preserving a sense of the ultimacy of God. Vice versa, as we realize the ultimacy of God and transcend the finite, the concreteness that fosters our concern, recognition, and understanding is diminished, yielding a terrible sense of mystery disconnected from the existential situation in which we find ourselves. In short, the inherent tension of ultimate concern is also the inherent tension of the doctrine of God.[2]

---

[1] Paul Tillich, *Systematic Theology*, 3 vols. (Chicago: University of Chicago Press, 1951–1963) 1:211.

[2] Of course, Tillich actually presses much further than what I have outlined here. Speaking in some of his most sweepingly broad terms, Tillich further affirms that it is the projection of divine symbols and images onto this framework of ultimate concern that itself constitutes a "religious" phenomenon. Moreover, this concept of ultimate concern is fundamental to how Tillich conceptualizes the existential quality of humankind's relation to God's ultimacy as faith: whereby faith is the ecstatic act of the entire personality surrendering to the identified concern in its intended ultimacy. See Tillich, *Systematic Theology*, 1:212; and *Dynamics of Faith* (New York: Harper-Collins, 1957) 1–10, 122–23.

Broadly speaking, what we claim regarding ultimate concern, we can apply—in more classic theological language—to the doctrine of God.

This overarching structure (connecting language of ultimate concern to insights regarding the doctrine of God) shapes the second part of the first volume of Tillich's *Systematic Theology*. For the time being, I set Tillich's connection between ultimate concern and the doctrine of God aside. Instead, I will focus on the robust phenomenological descriptions Tillich offers regarding ultimate concern, while always bearing in mind the critical idea of ultimate concern's inner tension: the ultimacy of a concern is perpetually self-negating the concreteness of the concern.

In these phenomenological descriptions, we find ultimate concern intimately tied to Tillich's notion of the existential and the holy. With regard to both the existential and the holy, he notes a concern is holy or existential as it describes participation transcending the cleavage between subjectivity and objectivity that is fundamental to Tillich's four-fold ontology.[3] Using the language of self and world, Tillich identifies a constant interplay between the self as more typically imagined and the *self that experiences itself in the midst of a world*. This second sense can be difficult to conceptualize. It is the self understood wholly in terms of the "unity of manifoldness" to which the self belongs. More succinctly, he is claiming the self *has* and is *had* by a world.[4]

Symbols of ultimate concern are holy or existential to the extent that they trouble the self-world or subject-object division in this polarity: they blur *having* and *being had*. Tillich is more specific, however, about how this troubling occurs. An ultimate concern is able to transcend this subject-object divide to the extent that it

---

[3] Tillich, *Systematic Theology*, 1:168, 214, 216; *Dynamics of Faith*, 11–14.
[4] Tillich, *Systematic Theology*, 1:170.

correlates to the infinite. A legitimate or functional expression of ultimate concern is one in which the ultimate concern gives depth and meaning to all other penultimate concerns, giving direction and a sense of centeredness to the whole personality that might well be characterized as faith. "Faith…is not a matter of the mind in isolation, or of the soul in contrast to mind and body, or of the body (in the sense of animal faith), but is the centered movement of the whole personality toward something of ultimate meaning and significance."[5] This centered movement towards wholeness characterizes the holy or the existential transcending a subject-object or self-world separation.

Nonetheless, it is critical to understand that the wholeness sought is not a simple union of self and world without distinction. Here the separating, disjunctive tension that characterizes our experience of self and world in existence is overcome. Ultimate concern represents an integrating power, whereby the various polarities characterizing the remainder of Tillich's ontology come toward a union that never loses the presupposed differences of the polarities.[6] In contrast to a legitimate ultimate concern expressing the holy or the existential, false ultimacy is identified by the finite claiming to be infinite (i.e., when the concreteness of a concern falsely claims to be ultimate itself instead of being symbolic for the ultimate).[7] False ultimacy annihilates the distinction of self and world in order to overcome the existential tension therein.

Stepping away from the more technical phenomenological description of ultimate concern for a moment, we also find that

---

[5] Tillich, *Dynamics of Faith*, 123.

[6] In various places we find Tillich names this overcoming "love." See ibid., 129–35; and *Love, Power, and Justice* (Oxford; New York: Oxford University Press, 1954) ch. 7.

[7] Tillich, *Dynamics of Faith*, 13–18.

Tillich refers to this false ultimacy or poor ultimate concern as that which is idolatrous, and he further claims that justice can resist idolatry. His account of justice and idolatry parallels his account of the distinction between authentic and false ultimacy. Justice judges the tendency of any particular concern to destroy the centered personality of the individual who in faith surrenders to a particular concern. In echoing the language above, a false ultimacy, or idolatry, proposes a simple union of self and world that annihilates the tension between these polar terms instead of overcoming their disjunction as with an authentic, or just, ultimate concern. The parallelism suggests justice and ultimate concern are commensurate ideas in Tillich's work. *The claim being made is that the pursuit of justice expresses a way of being that resists the self-annihilation of idolatry and promotes the wholeness of a centered personality as it is fostered by participation in a holy or existential concern that is directed toward the ultimacy characterized by transcending the separation of subject-object or self-world dichotomies.*[8] To put it as simply as possible, justice is a criterion for discerning the difference between legitimate ultimate concern and false ultimacies.

We can deepen this connection between justice and ultimate concern by turning to Tillich's short work, *Love, Power, and Justice.* Herein, he identifies four principles that comprise his vision of justice: adequacy, equality, personality, and liberty.[9] Adequacy refers to the correlation of form and content: the way in which we pursue justice cannot violate the justice we intend to promote. In terms of the language of the holy, the adequacy principle suggests

---

[8] Tillich, *Systematic Theology,* 1:216; and *Dynamics of Faith,* 28.

[9] Tillich is quick to admit that there is no way of mechanically prescribing principles that will guarantee justice in all situations; however, he suggests his principles should apply in all situations that seek the reunion of the separated. See Tillich, *Love, Power, and Justice,* 55–56.

justice must be pursued in a form that never inhibits the actualization of the holy. Tillich identifies that adequacy is most often violated when laws outlive their usefulness (i.e., when laws inadvertently create systems of injustice because, while adequate in the past, they no longer promote justice in the present). The final three principles are all strongly interrelated. Equality is the dignity due any person as one who, admittedly partially, actualizes the power of being. Personality refers to the need for justice to treat people as ends and not means. It is to respect and support the power of any person to pursue a sense of ultimate concern. Finally, liberty is the principle referring to the preservation of freedom and self-determination that is fundamental to enacting personality. I would relate these four principles by suggesting that no form of justice is adequate so long as the forms of that justice do not promote equality, personality, and liberty.[10]

Now, we might apply these four principles to guide our interpretation of both what and how holy or existential concerns might justly claim symbolically to manifest ultimacy. In a simple, additive fashion, we could claim that legitimate ultimate concern would develop the unity of wholeness between self and world (a unity that avoids any totalizing collapse that eliminates distinction between these poles) while promoting a sense of justice characterized by adequacy, equality, personality, and liberty.

Adequacy, equality, personality, and liberty would be minimum criteria for discerning a wise expression of ultimate concern, because in following Tillich's own work in his *Systematic Theology*, a further distinction arises. He suggests distinguishing religious symbols that possess some truth from those that are true according to the principles of justice: "A religious symbol possesses some

---

[10] Ibid., 57–62.

truth if it adequately expresses the correlation of revelation in which some person stands. A religious symbol *is* true if it adequately expresses the correlation of some person with final revelation."[11] A concern symbolically reveals the ultimate either partially or entirely depending on its correlation to *final revelation* within the *Systematic Theology*. Final revelation is that which is unsurpassable—a revelatory criterion that norms all others. To be final, such a revelation must survive the power of negating itself, becoming completely transparent to that which it reveals. This happens through being united with the ground of being in surrendering the finitude of a symbol in order to be transparent to the infinite that is being-itself.[12]

At the end of the chapter, I will briefly turn to Tillich's final lecture in order to consider how it might qualify this concept of "final revelation" and what that could mean for understanding how justice serves as a minimal criterion for discerning ultimate concern. On its strictest interpretation, though, I am suggesting that we can use Tillich's own work to provide a means by which we can assess how *bodies* may or may not be of ultimate concern or manifest ultimate concern (as religious symbols). I would phrase this in terms of three questions: (1) do bodies provide a means of evidencing unity between self and world; (2) does the analysis of such bodies support the four principles of justice; and (3) does the analysis of bodies adequately express final revelation? After analyzing cyborg bodies, we can use these three questions in order to evaluate how a cyborg body might or might not be our ultimate concern.

---

[11] Tillich, *Systematic Theology*, 1:240.
[12] Tillich, *Systematic Theology*, 1:132–33.

CYBORG BODIES

What is critical to contemporary discourse about cyborgs is a characterization of the activity and interplay between human beings and technology that troubles conceptions of individual agency.[13] With the cyborg, there is a blurring of the boundary between organism and machine. This blurriness opens up new freedoms and manifestations of agency, forcing us to question fundamental aspects of human autonomy.[14] The important point here is that if we think deeply through the implications of hybridity in the cyborg, then human bodies are decentered. The stable, fixed notion of a "natural" body separate from its world, bounding what is legitimately me (subject) as distinct from everything else (object), is antiquated in light of the post-human.

Instead, discourse on the cyborg follows the question that Donna Haraway asks so provocatively in her "Cyborg Manifesto": "Why should our bodies end at the skin or include at best other beings encapsulated by skin?"[15] Thinking with cyborg bodies calls for a recognition of an "attunement" whereby the body incorporates something from the world around it. I think of my daughter learning to swing a baseball bat. At first, the bat is foreign to her: an object in the world that stands against her body. Gradually,

---

[13] My work is making use of a critical distinction between post-humanist and transhumanist accounts of cyborg hybridity. See Jeanine Thweatt-Bates, *Cyborg Selves: A Theological Anthropology of the Post-Human*, Ashgate Science and Religion (Farnham; Burlington: Ashgate, 2012). Parts of this section of the paper also appear in a different format in Adam Pryor, *Body of Christ Incarnate for You: Conceptualizing God's Desire for the Flesh*, Studies in Body and Religion Series (Lanham: Lexington, 2016) ch. 7.

[14] Thweatt-Bates, *Cyborg Selves*, 19.

[15] Donna Haraway, "A Cyborg Manifesto: Science, Technology, and Socialist-Feminism in the Late Twentieth Century," in *Simians, Cyborgs, and Women: The Reinvention of Nature* (New York: Routledge, 1991) 178.

with practice and time, she has come to swing the bat more naturally: to experience it as an extension of her arms and hands in hitting a baseball.

Still, there is something lacking in this example. The hybridity of the cyborg forms an *indelibly shaping relationship* with technology that is highly somatic.[16] While my daughter may put down the bat when she is done playing baseball, cyborg hybridity calls for a more permanent fixture in this incorporation to the body. The permanence or fusion that is a part of this cyborg hybridity can resonate with Haraway's insight that incarnation is prosthetic.[17] The key is to recognize that our bodies are not natural phenomena inscribing natural wholeness, but what Sharon Betcher calls "prosthetic erratics": a stitching together of body and machine unconstrained by unspoken normativity that marks the use of prosthetics to reestablish a mythical wholeness.[18]

Disability theology is a critical dialogue partner in this regard as it looks to those who take up prostheses each day; it consistently draws the cyborg futurist back from any transcendent dream of enhancing the body towards the realization of some (mythical) perfect body.[19] As Nancy Eiesland well realizes, "Unless the notion of embodiment is deliberately deconstructed, the cultural norms of 'body as natural' seep into the subtext" and we can lose sight of

---

[16] Thweatt-Bates, *Cyborg Selves*, 142–49. Her reconfiguring of Wesley Wildman's metaphor for human beings as "walking, thinking ecologies" is particularly apt. See also Wesley J. Wildman, "Distributed Identity: Human Beings as Walking, Thinking Ecologies in the Microbial World," in *Human Identity at the Intersection of Science, Technology, and Religion,* ed. Nancey Murphy and Christopher C. Knight (Burlington: Ashgate, 2010) 165–66.

[17] Haraway, "A Cyborg Manifesto," 180.

[18] Sharon V. Betcher, *Spirit and the Politics of Disablement* (Minneapolis: Fortress Press, 2007) 102ff.

[19] Thweatt-Bates, *Cyborg Selves*, 155ff.

"the 'mixed blessing' of the body in the real, lived experience of people with disabilities" who help us imagine how to "explicitly deconstruct any norms which are part of the unexpressed agenda of 'normal embodiment.'"[20]

Eiesland's examination of the narratives of Dianne DeVries and Nancy Mairs remains helpful in pursuing this end.[21] For both DeVries and Mairs, the presentation of their body space includes devices and technologies that confound any sense of a normalizing body pattern. For DeVries this took the shape of persistently re-jecting prosthetic devices from childhood that facilitated the "normalcy" of bipedal, upright movement in favor of functional devices. As Eiesland aptly notes, DeVries is truly subversive with her subtle linguistic shifts: referring to the battery pack for her wheelchair as her legs or moving her wheelchair as walking.[22] For Mairs this incorporation is slightly different and she describes it developmentally, which matches the progressive changes to her

---

[20] Nancy Eiesland, *The Disabled God: Toward a Liberatory Theology of Disability* (Nashville: Abingdon Press, 1994) 22.

[21] "[T]he narratives highlight an alternative understanding of em-bodiment, recognizing it as an intricate interweaving of physical sensa-tions and emotional attachments, irrespective of socially constructed no-tions of 'normal' bodies or 'appropriate' relations. DeVries and Mairs include as integral parts of their bodies braces and wheelchairs. Both rely on close relationships to increase their own sense of body. Their experi-ences reveal painstaking processes of putting themselves together using whatever resources that are available. In contrast to romantic notions of 'natural' embodiment, both discuss embodying technology. Some devic-es—for example, wheelchairs and braces—are integrated into their body awareness, while other appliances that frustrate their sense of body are rejected" (ibid., 47).

[22] Ibid., 37–38; referencing Geyla Frank, "On Embodiment: A Case Study of Congenital Limb Deficiency in American Culture," in *Women with Disabilities*, ed. M. Fine and A. Asch (Philadelphia: Temple Uni-versity Press, 1988) 51.

body space that accompany multiple sclerosis. In her account, there is not so much adaption and linguistic subversion of normalizing body patterns, but a concentration on the lived experience of how her own body incorporates "insensate" technologies and what this reveals about human experience. Here, too, though, the bodily awareness is tied to functional adaptation—physical and social adaptation.[23]

What these examples illustrate is that the body is mutable; a natural wholeness or senses of normativity cannot describe the body well. The body space does not stop at the skin, cordoned off from the environment and technologies around it. The body is cyborg; its incarnation is prosthetic as it incorporates technologies that augment functionality in the world around it. Moreover, this incorporation is not limited to ambulatory and mechanical devices. In light of the highly technological features the cyborg brings to mind, speech-generating devices or other communication devices for ALS patients, referred to as Augmentative/Alternative Communication (AAC), can be a good example for imagining this same issue of the incorporative body space as it relates to something more technologically complex.

The most common AAC for an ALS patient includes a "switch" controlled by tiny movements that allows the user to select letters or basic words from an onscreen keyboard, which can then subsequently be sent to a speech synthesizer. Current research may even make the switch obsolete for such AAC devices, given the success of brain-computer interfaces, such as the Berlin Brain-Computer Interface (BBCI). The BBCI uses an electroen-

---

[23] Eiesland, *The Disabled God*, 43–44; referencing Nancy Mairs, *Carnal Acts* (New York: HarperCollins, 1990) 111; and *Ordinary Time: Cycles in Marriage, Faith, and Renewal* (Boston: Beacon Press, 1993) 167–68.

cephalogram (EEG) monitoring bonnet to calibrate itself to well-honed neural motor competencies of the individual wearing it. In effect, one can imagine limb movement that stimulates neuronal firing detected by the EEG bonnet and translated into equivalent manipulation of an electronic medium. The BBCI in particular is important because it is working to decrease training times for users of the interface technology as well as make the technology more adaptable to issues regarding brain-signal variability (both between various trials and between various users).[24]

The applications here are tremendous in terms of therapeutic value. Imagine an ALS patient one day being able to move herself or communicate by simply imagining the movement of limbs. This would provide a therapy that does not involve long training time for use, but draws on the well-established motor neural pathways she has already developed.

Even with switch-based AACs, these devices are excellent and recognizable examples of medical cyborgs. The device itself is highly visible, personalizable (Stephen Hawking copyrighted his voice), and the freedom and possibilities they affect are quite dramatic (enabling communication with other human beings that before would have been impossible or far more difficult). There is a blurring of the machine/human boundary as the body incorporates this technology to itself; the organism and machine hybridize.

The examples that I have offered above with AACs and prostheses are quite visible instances of cyborg hybridity, but the blur-

---

[24] Benjamin Blankertz et al., "The Non-Invasive Berlin Brain-Computer Interface: Fast Acquisition of Effective Performance in Untrained Subjects," *NeuroImage* 37/2 (15 Aug. 2007): 539–50; and "The Berlin Brain-Computer Interface: Non-Medical Uses of BCI Technology," *Frontiers in Neuroscience* 4 (8 Dec. 2010): 1–17.

ring of the machine-human boundary occurs in subtler but pervasive ways as well—both inside and outside of medical technologies. Remaining in medical technologies for the moment, we
might consider permanent surgical mesh used in hernia repair sur-
geries. As the permanent mesh fuses with the body, it enables enhanced mobility and faster recovery offering otherwise unimagined
freedoms. However, a fundamental dependence on the mesh as a
visceral incorporation of a technology cannot be denied. The key
point is that the human enhancement of cyborg hybridity should
be something very familiar to nearly anyone with access to contemporary medical technology; it is not limited to the more visible
example of prostheses or complex technologies like AACs.

Appreciating the importance of this hybridity, however, requires a shift in beliefs about the incorporation of technology in
order to embrace the idea of cyborg existence. In this regard, the
critical critique offered by Sharon Betcher of the cyborg is invaluable. Speaking from her own experience with leg prostheses, she
observes the body patterns that the cyborg all too often reinforces.
As she eloquently puts it,

> That this unveiling (of the donut hole of my limb loss), ra-
> ther than the curious, cosmetically covered endoskeletal
> structure standing in for my leg, should throw off the light
> switch of desire is a clue for me that Haraway's analysis may
> be slightly off course. When considering inclusion among the
> human community, the cyborg's machine/human interface
> seems not to be as troubling as a prosthetically unprosthely-
> tized body—a disabled body refusing social comeliness or
> seemliness.[25]

If the prosthetic limb covers over a social disgust and discom-

---

[25] Betcher, *Spirit and the Politics of Disablement*, 97.

fort, then Betcher fears that thinking about the cyborg inadvertently reinscribes a sense of bodily holism and wholesomeness. Betcher admits this is certainly not an *organic* wholeness, but she rightfully fears that the fusion of organism and machine covers, instead of *dis*covers, the somatic realities and discourses of *real* bodies using prosthetics most akin to her notion of the cyborg.[26] Betcher's critique is critical to keep in mind because the hybridity of the cyborg will be lost if the technology with which we are fused is merely passive: if nature and technology are even remotely thought of as tools to approximate a prevenient wholeness or even a means of enhancing a natural wholeness, then we simply return to a social problematic about what counts as natural and how the use of these tools does or does not accord with that naturalness. How, then, can we think of this technology as an active partner in the hybridization of cyborg bodies?

To get at this question, we can think of an early technology for human beings: shoes. Putting on shoes prevents us from cutting our feet while traveling; they allow us to walk longer distances more comfortably; and they are a technology that has been readily adapted by human beings for millennia. The technology incorporates to our bodies—on a very regular basis in many places in the world. Yet, in common-sense parlance, we would not often say that we are "hybridized" with our shoes. They are a technological tool, but not something fused with who we are as cyborgs.

Why is it so clearly commonsense to treat technology as *merely* a tool? Certainly answering this question is itself the subject of many books, but I would suggest in brief that part of the persistence of this commonsense notion relates to the assumption that we do not often perceive technology as active. We usually construe

---

[26] Ibid., 99.

technology as a passive feature of the world around us: a tool on which human use inscribes meaning. The shoe is not active because it is a tool whose objective meaning is limited by its passive relation to the active meaning-formation of a subject with consciousness that is radically distinct from it. Subject and object are made radically distinct; the dumb shoe and the conscious agent are rendered as perpetually distinct no matter how frequent or long-lasting their interactions. What we begin to see is that there cannot be hybridization or mixture (as with cyborg hybridization) where there is not, at least subversively, an active element spanning the multiple features being hybridized.[27]

The technological enhancement of cyborg bodies must have implications for a wider breakdown of traditional boundaries re-

---

[27] We could argue that the previous example of the AAC of an ALS patient appears more active, more engaging, a less inscribed technological tool than our passive shoes; and, we could further argue that there is a gradation of activity passivity in these technological-biological mergers. An AAC is nearly active, but prostheses are not quite as active as the AAC, and shoes are practically passive because their facilitation of movement is not as limb-like as the prosthesis. The problem with such an argument is it limits the "active" quality of these technological-biological mergers to those that are most akin to features classically attributed to the mind (like the speech device) and make passive those features that only passively conform to the body (the shoes)—leaving the functional control over prostheses somewhere in between. In short, such an argument reinscribes a mind/body dualism wherein all the technological-biological mergers of the cyborg occur with passive technology, but it appears more active the more clearly the technology engages the classic features of mind in the biological subject. Of course, the problem here is that this makes the body a passive vessel like the technology in the midst of the world; on such a view the body is just a repository for the mind—and the technological-biological merger of the cyborg is really just a cipher for the same mind/body problem that has plagued philosophy since Descartes. See, for instance, Elizabeth Grosz, *Volatile Bodies: Toward a Corporeal Feminism*, Theories of Representation and Difference (Bloomington: Indiana University Press, 1994).

configuring conceptions of human subjectivity and environment. "This reconfiguration of human subjectivity through the increasing integration of self and environment makes this technological-biological merger an ontological, not merely practical, matter."[28] On such an interpretation, the reconfiguring hybridity of the cyborg is no mere adiaphora. Cyborg hybridity skews our well-bounded concepts of distinctive, active, conscious subjects and common, passive, mute objects. Taking seriously cyborg hybridity entails a critique of our conceptualization of environment or "nature" as partner in thinking about cyborg bodies.

For the cyborg, nature is not a simple given. Nature is instead a socially constructed category that *poses* as absolute, thereby forming the norms and practices that shape our lives.[29] Here, the natural is not some mythical absolute to which we can make unquestionable appeal. Instead, the material world is an active partner in co-constructive relationship with human beings because, as Anne Kull observes, categories—such as culture and nature—are "consequences," not "causes."[30] The cyborg incorporation of technologies points to a reconceptualization of the way we interact with the world around us, such that we do not have a relationship with some pure, pristine notion of nature as that which is untouched by humankind. The artificial and the natural blur as the cyborg interacts with the material world; or, as cyborg theorists often describe it, the cyborg interacts with "technonature."[31] When the world of the cyborg is no longer "nature" romantically conceived, but tech-

---

[28] Thweatt-Bates, *Cyborg Selves*, 21.

[29] Ibid., 29.

[30] Anne Kull, "The Cyborg as an Interpretation of Culture-Nature," *Zygon* 36/1 (March 2001): 56.

[31] On technonature, see the especially helpful work of Anne Kull in her article "Speaking Cyborg: Technoculture and Technonature," *Zygon* 37/2 (June 2002): 279–87.

nonature, an interesting shift occurs: the cyborg no longer subverts the natural (as an assumed normative category). When all nature is technonature, the technologically adapted body of the cyborg, somewhat surprisingly, becomes most natural.[32]

Even with this shift from nature to technonature, we have not yet addressed how technonature is active. How are machines "strangely lively," and why has this idea been resonant for so many thinkers?[33] The cyborg body incorporates technonature. It incorporates plastic and carbon fiber as prostheses, the hair-trigger switches of ACCs, the simple technologies and complex portable technologies of all kinds for human enhancement. These incorporations are truly a "taking-in" of technonature to the space of cyborg bodies.

Still, even this radically intimate action of incorporation does not make the cyborg body contiguous with technonature. There is not a merger but a hybridity. Even in the proximity of hybridity there is a separation—a distance without which the proximity would not be possible and only fusion would occur. There remains a fundamental space between a cyborg body and technonature; this space points to the active quality of technonature. The incorporated technologies are neither merely a tool of technoscientific production nor a passive instrument ready for a human subject to inscribe constructivist meanings upon them. Instead, posthumanist accounts of the cyborg affirm an understanding of technonature as a tricky agent with which our bodies reveal tentative and shifting relationships that are formative for our world and

---

[32] Donna Haraway, "The Promises of Monsters: A Regenerative Politics for Inappropriate/d Others," in *Cultural Studies*, ed. Lawrence Grossberg, Cary Nelson, and Paula A. Treichler (New York: Routledge, 1992) 152.

[33] Haraway, "A Cyborg Manifesto," 151.

ourselves.

HOLY CYBORG BODIES

At this point, it is clear that post-humanist accounts of the cyborg offer a vision of human being that blurs hard distinctions between subject and object or between self and world. The blurring is not a fusion of body and technonature; there is a preserved distance as the incorporated technology and the organic body remain distinguishable parts of the cyborg. However, the incorporation of such a technology is not a mere adaption of a tool either. The cyborg body is a hybrid that incorporates technologies, thereby opening up new freedoms and agency for the individual who incorporates said technology.

Insofar as the cyborg body opens new avenues to unity that span the distance between self and world, the cyborg body is, or at least potentially is according to Tillich's model, a symbol that can reveal ultimate concern insofar as it is transcending this cleavage of self and world. If we understand the technologies of cyborg bodies as more than mere tools grafted to otherwise "natural" bodies, we can think of the hybridity exemplified by the cyborg as what Tillich would call a "centering movement of our personality." Playing with both the cyborg theorist and Tillichian languages employed throughout this chapter, we can claim the cyborg body models centering as a faithful action that lovingly unifies self and technonature. The cyborg body is, then, a holy concern directed toward a sense of ultimacy characterized by the transcendence of the separation of self and world. The cyborg body is a valid ultimate concern.

An ultimate concern should not violate the four principles of justice, however, and it is far from self-evident that the cyborg incorporation of technology will always work in such a justice-oriented and personality-centering way. Science fiction media provides a variety of dystopias that illustrate this ambiguity: conceiving of cyborg bodies that conflict with the Tillichian criteria of justice or are a far cry from centering our personalities. The cyberpunk themed *Deus Ex* series has played with this theme most prominently, exploring the ethical problematic of human augmentation in terms of public safety, the influence of corporations and transnational entities, and problems of bigotry and alienation between cyborg bodies and natural human beings.

Just as the cyborg might function in a holy vein in its utopian or hopeful rendering, the dystopic, negative connotations reveal the monstrous side of the cyborg. This monstrous cyborg is not only the subject of science fiction. Consider Google Glass. The 5 Point bar in Seattle banned the device before it was even available to the public, and Sarah Slocum now famously had her Google Glass taken from her face, as recounted by a YouTube video she uploaded, at Molotov's in San Francisco.[34] What seemingly countless blog posts and news articles have noted is a low-level suspicion, which at times erupted into mild violence, over Glass violating the privacy of others. The technology has even generated its own slang to describe this phenomenon: glasshole.

While some might argue that, even in the case of Google Glass, we do not have a true cyborg because of the removable quality of the technology, Grindfests and other biohacking events have made what once seemed like science-fiction-style integration of technologies a contemporary reality. Described in detail through the biohack.me forums, most often at these events people

---

[34] Casey Newton, "Seattle Dive Bar Becomes First to Ban Google Glass," *CNET*, 8 March 2013, http://www.cnet.com/news/seattle-dive-bar-becomes-first-to-ban-google-glass/; and Anisse Gross, "What's the Problem with Google Glass?" *The New Yorker*, 4 March 2014, http://www.newyorker.com/business/currency/whats-the-problem-with-google-glass.

inject glass-encased RFID chips, sometimes with Near Field Communication (NFC) antennae, between their thumb and forefinger or insert small magnets (such as the m31 designed for this purpose) into fingertips.[35] The effects and reasons for these types of body modification are quite diverse. In the case of inserting magnets into the fingertips, often such cyborgs describe a "sixth sense" whereby the magnet allows one to feel electro-magnetic fields in a way that creates a new sensible relationship with electrically powered objects. Neil Harbisson, the self-identified cyborg artist, has famously pursued an extreme version of such perception modification. He has an antenna attached to a vibrating chip inside his skull that allows him to transpose colors and sounds. With this new mode of perception, he has created sonochromatic portraits and painted speeches.[36]

On the RFID chip side of biohacking, chip-programmed implants allow the user to perform simple tasks with the wave of a hand. YouTube videos of biohackers opening electronic locks and starting modified cars with the wave of a hand are ubiquitous. More controversially, one such chipped-cyborg, Seth Wahle, has demonstrated the hacking potential of such incorporated devices by hacking android phones that came within a specific distance of the chip in his hand.[37]

---

[35] For a first-person description, see Dylan Matthews, "I Got a Computer Chip Implanted into My Hand. Here's How It Went.," *Vox*, 11 September 2015, http://www.vox.com/2015/9/11/9307991/ biohacking-grinders-rfid-implant.

[36] For instance, see Dann Berg, "I Have a Magnet Implant in My Finger," *Gizmodo*, accessed 24 May 2016, http://gizmodo.com/ 5895555/i-have-a-magnet-implant-in-my-finger; and Stuart Jeffries, "Neil Harbisson: The World's First Cyborg Artist," *The Guardian*, 6 May 2014, http://www.theguardian.com/artanddesign/2014/may/06/ neil-harbisson-worlds-first-cyborg-artist.

[37] See Rose Eveleth, "The Man Who Hacks Phones with an Im-

Cyborg biohacking can be quite diverse, though, moving beyond RFID chips and magnets. Grindhouse Wetware provides, perhaps, the clearest example. The group describes itself as "a dedicated team working towards a common goal—augmenting humanity using safe, affordable, open-source technology."[38] Implantables, such as the North Star or Circadia, use LED lights placed under the skin to indicate information about direction (North Star) or health metrics (Circadia). The second version of the North Star should include Bluetooth capability that will allow the cyborg to control devices with hand movements alone.[39] While these enhancements are certainly more integrated and less removable than wearables such as Google Glass, we can imagine going one step further with technology such as the brain-computer interfaces used as an example above.

The implications of BCIs are not only therapeutic. The neural monitoring that the Berlin Brain Computer Interface allows could have other applications. For instance, a BCI could evaluate performance capability with repetitive tasks and assess cognitive workload. It could also certainly have implications for a variety of media applications involving brain-computer interface controls.[40]

---

plant Under His Skin," *BBC*, 15 May 2015, http://www.bbc.com/future/story/20150515-i-hack-phones-with-touch-alone.

[38] "Grindhouse Wetware," accessed 24 May 2016, http://www.grindhousewetware.com/.

[39] Cadie Thompson, "Grindhouse Wetware Launches New Implantable Northstar Device," *Tech Insider*, 9 November 2015, http://www.techinsider.io/grindhouse-wetware-launches-new-implantable-northstar-device-2015-11.

[40] Blankertz et al., "The Berlin Brain-Computer Interface: Non-Medical Uses of BCI Technology," sect. 3 and 4. See also Michael Bensch et al., "Nessi: An EEG-Controlled Web Browser for Severely Paralyzed Patients," *Computational Intelligence and Neuroscience* 2007 (2007).

In any case, BCIs could eventually become a wearable technology with easily imaginable wide uses. Perhaps we will have a baseball cap that simply allows you to think and send that text message you previously had to type; a fedora and glasses for browsing the web at the speed of thought; or a beanie that writes lecture notes on a tablet for you as you simply think about your hand making the letters. If implantables were to become more mainstream, perhaps we could even imagine a far-future scenario where such BCI capabilities are a commonplace augmentation of traditional brain functioning.[41]

Do these cyborg bodies violate principles of justice? In such dystopic visions as with the *Deus Ex* science-fiction narrative, the four principles of justice are clearly violated. This dystopian sci-fi fantasy traipses across themes of liberty repeatedly. Although it has addressed liberty in unexpected ways, in the most recent iteration of the game the abject bodies are the cyborg bodies that lose freedom as their grafted technologies are hacked. In the real-world examples, issues relating to adequacy and equality become critical principles that limit the potential of these cyborg bodies to reveal ultimate concern. Equality, for instance, is particularly problematic. Global distribution of access to incorporative technologies that we would associate with cyborgs is wildly unequal. This alone may constitute a fundamental hindrance to conceiving of the cyborg body in terms of ultimate concern because the problem of access creates a fundamental disruption in the social fabric between the body of the cyborg and non-augmented, "natural" human bodies.[42]

---

[41] For an extended thought experiment that takes up how this idea might be a future trajectory of human being, see Yuval Noah Harari, *Homo Deus: A Brief History of Tomorrow* (New York NY: Harper, 2017).

[42] By contrast, one could argue that the technological enhancement of cyborg bodies inherently tends towards the four principles of justice so long as the intention of the technological enhancement is always directed towards

Keeping this in mind, we can now put the question cyborg bodies present more sharply: *does the cyborg manifest a holy body unifying self and technonature, or a terrifying, uncanny violation of the wholeness of the self?* That the cyborg presents to us with such ambiguity indicates that it is truly *monstrous*. In his book *Strangers, Gods, and Monsters*, Richard Kearney examines these liminal phenomena that are both awe-ful and awful. Following the work of Timothy Beal quite closely, Kearney suggests, "[T]he monster is not only a portent of impurity (the root of *monstrum* in *monere*, to warn) but also an apparition of something utterly other and numinous (from the root *monstrare*, to show)."[43]

Phenomenologically, the monstrous cyborg presents as a stranger; an uncanny figure, who is simultaneously familiar and unfamiliar, standing at the very threshold of my sensibilities. In her familiarity the stranger is a foreigner; someone who can be placed as a kind of person, even if that placement is utterly dissimilar to my own sense of self. But, in her unfamiliarity the stranger is an Other, someone who defies any category of placement—an utter alterity.[44]

The monstrous cyborg is a curious stranger. Before the human body that divorces itself from technonature, the cyborg is a foreigner. I recognize the cyborg body in its natural immediacy even if its incorporation of technonature is horrific to me. It is this

---

eschatological flourishing, as with Tomislav Mimetic, "Human Becoming," *Theology and Science*, 13/4 (Nov. 2015): 433–35.

[43] Richard Kearney, *Strangers, Gods, and Monsters: Interpreting Otherness* (London; New York: Routledge, 2003) 34. See also Timothy Beal, *Religion and Its Monsters* (London; New York: Routledge, 2001).

[44] See Kearney, *Strangers, Gods, and Monsters*, 67; and Richard Kearney and Kascha Semonovitch, eds., "At the Threshold: Foreigners, Strangers, Others," in *Phenomenologies of the Stranger: Between Hostility and Hospitality* (New York: Fordham University Press, 2011) 3–29.

horrific incorporation of technonature that is utterly othering to me; this intertwining of cyborg body and technonature exceeds the categories with which I can place the cyborg in terms of the familiarly natural. What is curious here is that it is the *incorporative* quality of the cyborg—its violation of a "natural" otherness between self and world—that makes it other before the natural human body: in overcoming what is itself a peculiar otherness between self and world, the cyborg is made uncanny before the natural body—is made into an othering stranger.[45]

If we begin to coalesce the language of Tillich, post-humanism, and the monstrous, we find that the cyborg is truly the monstrous stranger. The cyborg is holy in its non-totalizing unification of self and world; but in this capacity, it remains alterior so long as a strong conception of "nature" and the "natural human body" is maintained. To the natural body that affirms a hard-and-fast self-world distinction, the cyborg must remain the other, an uncharacterizable strangeness. The foreign elements of the cyborg are not merely benign. They symbolize a monstrous alien: something of which we should be suspicious and resistant.

Whether awe-ful or awful, there is a hermeneutic of justice—if we follow Tillich—that needs to be used in discerning if the monstrous cyborg body can truly be a holy concern that expresses ultimacy. In those instances where the cyborg is just, no matter the prospect of awful terror that it might inspire, our concern for the

---

[45] It is worth considering if a fundamental revision of self and world is characteristic of all monstrous bodies or only the monstrous cyborg. While I have used the cyborg, which does reconfigure a sense of self and world, the question is important from the perspective of Tillich's theology because it is this feature of the cyborg that makes it the subject of holy concern. If other monstrous bodies did not call us towards a revised unity of self and world, they would not be the subject of ultimate concern as I suggest the cyborg can be.

cyborg body reveals an awe-ful sense of ultimacy.

Moreover, the argument can widen at this point well beyond cyborg bodies. We should expect that *any* body that overcomes the separation of self and world justly can be an appropriate subject of ultimate concern; and any body that can be such a subject is probably going to be a little bit monstrous—awe-ful and awful to our commonsense understanding of self and world.

A FINAL QUESTION ABOUT FINAL REVELATION

One point remains undiscussed. My analysis of Tillich concluded with three questions to ask of the cyborg body, and in the analysis so far we have addressed only the first two questions: does the cyborg body reveal a unity of self and world, and does it support the four principles of justice? Even if we grant that cyborg bodies are able, in at least some instances, to do both of these things, we still must consider the relationship of cyborg bodies to final revelation.

In this regard, cyborg bodies raise a question that we also might ask of *any* body analyzed under this framework: can any body serve as an ultimate concern given the fundamental ambiguity that characterizes all living things in their estranged existence from Tillich's perspective? Within the Tillichian language game, this is to ask can any body *be* true or does it always only *possess some* truth? The obvious answer seems to be no body can meet the standard for expressing ultimate concern; the fundamental ambiguity of estranged existence certainly prevents any cyborg body (and perhaps any body at all) from being transparent to the ground of being as the final revelation of an ultimate concern it entails. Yet, there is something unsettling about the way in which a symbol must negate itself (especially if this symbol is something living and personal) in order to become transparent to ultimate concern as a final revelation.

I am afraid there is no thoroughgoing solution to this issue if a strict sense of transparency to final revelation is maintained. As outlined by Tillich's *Systematic Theology*, it seems that *no* body could be of ultimate concern because of the need for self-negation to effect final revelation. Following the *Systematic Theology* closely (though we could point to other texts as well), I fear the reader may be disappointed. If the reader's hope for this volume was to discover an existing outline for an embodied theology hidden within Tillich's own work, one will always fall somewhat short. It is not there; an embodied theology of Tillich is one that takes up Tillich's themes and imagines how different forms the body may take push those themes further. An embodied theology of Tillich is one that must push beyond Tillich's own place on the boundaries to boundaries of our own times and places. To do this with credibility, though, requires thinking a bit about this issue of final revelation. While I will not solve this problem in the conclusion of this chapter, I can imagine three distinct paths that draw on insights of Tillich for formulating an embodied theology of ultimate concern in light of the self-negation of final revelation.

First, one can imagine the aspirations of the cyborg body as akin to the eschatological hope of Tillich's vision of essentialization, more than being akin to the body as he conceptualizes it in terms of existential estrangement.[46] In essentialization the negative element that is entangled with our estranged existence is overcome by the uniting or drawing together of "the positive" with essential

---

[46] This is a variation on the phenomenological argument made in Johanne Stubbe-Teglbjærg Kristensen's *Body and Hope: A Constructive Interpretation of Recent Eschatology by Means of the Phenomenology of the Body* (Tübingen: Mohr Siebeck, 2013) 170–71, 267–70. She makes the argument in terms of Merleau-Ponty's notion of the flesh, but the relationship of cyborg to technonature is akin to the philosophical project she outlines.

being contributing to the fulfillment of the Kingdom of God. The cyborg body could serve as a kind of realized Tillichian eschatology: a reconceptualization of the relationship between self and world that so fundamentally challenges the presuppositions of Tillich's ontology that the cyborg body, when properly conceived in terms of its unity with technonature, is always a proper subject of ultimate concern because it seeks to realize in the present the essentialized hope of Tillich's understanding of new life. Yet to adopt such a position certainly would require questioning if this picture of ultimate wholeness in Tillich's essentialization can be made coherent with anything like the critique of holism in Betcher's questioning of the cyborg—a question of determining the function of the world in inscribing on the body what constitutes "legitimate" forms of wholeness. More work would need to be done to justify such a conclusion.

Second, one can simply reject the criterion of ultimate concern being transparent to final revelation and thereby account for cyborg bodies, and perhaps all holy bodies, as worthy of ultimate concern. Tillich's own writings may even support such a critique. On the one hand, if we look closely at Tillich's understanding of symbols, it seems that he was not truly pursuing the self-negation of transparency but something more like a translucency of the symbol: the symbol makes visible the otherwise invisible power of the ground of being.[47] Alternatively, one might claim that given his final lecture, where Tillich critiques his own systematic investigation of theology, his notion of a "religion of the concrete spirit" cannot be conceived as having something properly termed "final"

---

[47] I have argued for such an understanding of symbol elsewhere. See Adam Pryor, "Comparing Tillich and Rahner on Symbol: Evidencing the Modernist/Postmodernist Boundary," *Bulletin of the North American Paul Tillich Society* 37/2 (Spring 2011): 23–38.

revelation. His advocating for a vision of God operating "within religion against religion" opens up a notion of the holy in religious phenomena where what is final is the continual resistance of demonization that opens up our sense of spiritual freedom. In either case, a classic sense of final, definitive revelation to which all other events of revelation are compared as foundational seems to be rejected.[48]

Third, one might make use of a Kierkegaardian distinction for a variation of the second approach outlined directly above. Perhaps we could call the cyborg body (and other bodies as well insofar as they seek to justly overcome the polarization of self and world) an "indirect communication" of ultimate concern. Søren Kierkegaard distinguishes direct and indirect communication quite clearly. Direct communication conveys knowledge; indirect communication conveys a capability. What if what is at stake in conveying ultimate concern is not the transparency of self-negation as with final revelation, but indirect communication of the just pursuit of a unity of self and world? The cyborg body could be such an indirect communication—expressing a just, loving unification of self and world that is intended to inspire the capability of other bodies towards this pursuit. In a sense, this is an addendum to Tillich's principle of adequacy reviewed above. Because the body is finite, an adequate representation of the eternality of ultimate concern requires indirect communication. The direct communication of a transparency to final revelation would be inadequate because it could not represent the eternal quality of final revelation; however, indirect communication through the body would be no less valuable a representation of ultimate concern than its direct communi-

---

[48] See Paul Tillich, "The Significance of the History of Religions for the Systematic Theologian," in *The Future of Religions*, ed. Jerald C. Brauer (New York: Harper & Row, 1966) 80–94.

cation through final revelation because the two modes of communication intend to convey different things.

While one might employ any of these approaches in order to deal with Tillich's concept of final revelation, I want to emphasize the richness of Tillich's theology as a resource for thinking theologically about the body. By drawing on his phenomenological investigation of the holy and existential concerns, Tillich provides a means—even if not realized in his own work—for thinking about the body as ultimate concern. Moreover, those bodies that appear to us in our everyday encounter with the world as strange and uncanny may be the best subject of our ultimate concern, when they do not violate the principles of justice, because they open new ways of imagining the unity between self and world. If this is the case, then an embodied theology of Tillich is one that entails a host of ethical injunctions to care ultimately for those bodies most at risk in society because they challenge our everyday thinking about self and world.

7

Tillich and Transhumanism

DEVAN STAHL

Amongst those who call themselves "Christian transhumanists," Paul Tillich is one of the most quoted theologians.[1] There are many obvious and not-so-obvious reasons why so-called Christian transhumanists find a kindred ally in Tillich. Tillich's method of correlation led him to be open to finding the latent spiritual depth of various secular projects, particularly when those pursuits were aimed at healing. For this reason, many see Tillich as a prime candidate to support the transhumanist movement from a Christian perspective, albeit posthumously. Although transhumanism began as a chiefly atheistic endeavor, some Christians now see it as a partner in the work of the Gospel, because transhumanism aims to overcome suffering and death. Whether or not Tillich would have found himself in agreement with the larger aims of the transhumanist movement, however, remains an open question. Tillich likely would have been skeptical of the transhumanist movement's telos, even if he may have found promise in some transhumanist technologies. Tillich's theology of culture, while deeply hopeful and open to the Spirit moving in forms outside the church, was

---

[1] See, for example, James McLean Ledford, "Prepare for HyperEvolution with Christian Transhumanism," last modified 9 December 2005, http://www.hyper-evolution.com/; and "Quotes," *Christian Transhumanist Association,* http://www.christiantranshumanism.org/quotes.

nevertheless wary of utopian fantasies that promised everlasting peace and security.

Tillich's writings on technology, science, and religion do not reveal him to be a strong supporter or opponent of any particular scientific movement that would resemble transhumanism. Tillich's firm belief in the ambiguity inherent in all human projects acts as a necessary caution for Christian transhumanists who wish to use Tillich's writings to support their cause. To show why Tillich would have resisted the label "Christian transhumanist," I first describe the overarching aims and underlying metaphysics of transhumanism, as well as its critics. Next, I examine Tillich's relationship to technology and his reactions to similarly inspired projects in the past as well as his understanding of religion, ultimate concern, and idolatry. I conclude that Tillich's notion of ambiguity resists a full adoption of the transhumanist movement. Beyond what Tillich would have thought of transhumanism or Christian transhumanism, there is reason for Christians to be cautious wholly adopting, rejecting, or ignoring the transhumanist agenda.

TRANSHUMANISM

To understand why Christian transhumanists reference Tillich, one must first understand the transhumanist movement. According to the Transhumanist Declaration, transhumanists, "…envision the possibility of broadening human potential by overcoming aging, cognitive shortcomings, involuntary suffering, and our confinement to planet Earth."[2] These are, of course, not modest goals—transhumanists want to cure human fragility and mortality. The result of overcoming aging and death will be a new

---

[2] Doug Baily et al., "Transhumanist Declaration," *Humanity+* (1998 [last modified March 2009]): http://humanityplus.org/philosophy/ transhumanist-declaration/.

kind of human being—a post-human. Post-humans will be "beings that have vastly greater capacity than present human beings have."[3] Transhumanists do not necessarily agree on the best way to achieve the post-human status, but most suspect the post-human will have a vastly different physiology than human beings, and may even have different values,[4] social relationships,[5] and modes of spirituality,[6] as well as enhanced intelligence and morality.[7] Transhumanists reject critiques they are "playing God, messing with nature, tampering with our human essence, or displaying punishable hubris,"[8] because they do not believe humans should be limited by evolution. Nor do transhumanists accept the classic therapy/enhancement divide, which separates the application of medical treatments that provide therapy to treat disease and deformity from interventions that enhance "normal" human traits.[9] The enhancement of our current state is the point of transhumanism and so it is morally indistinguishable from therapy. Only through enhancement can we escape the threats of aging and death.

There are at least three ways transhumanists believe they can achieve radical age extension and eventually immortality: through

---

[3] Nick Bostrom, "Transhumanist Values," in *Ethical Issues for the 21st Century*, ed. Frederick Adams (Charlottesville: Philosophical Documentation Center Press, 2005) 3–14.

[4] Bostrom, "Transhumanist Values," 8

[5] Ibid.

[6] Ray Kurzweil, *The Age of Spiritual Machines: When Computers Exceed Human Intelligence* (London: Penguin Books, 2000).

[7] Julian Savulescu and Ingmar Persson, "Moral Enhancement, Freedom, and the God Machine," *Monist* 95/3 (2012): 399–421.

[8] Bostrom, "Transhumanist Values," 4.

[9] For more on this debate, see L.Y. Cabrera, N.S. Fitz, and P.B. Reiner, "Empirical Support for the Moral Salience of the Therapy-Enhancement Distinction in the Debate Over Cognitive, Affective, and Social Enhancement," *Neuroethics* 8/3 (2015): 243–56.

super-machines, through cellular and genetic alterations, or through biotechnology enhancements. The first strategy is largely promoted by Ray Kurzweil, the major figure in the Singularity movement. Kurzweil believes one day, in the not-so-distant future, we will be able to upload our individual brains into superhuman machines.[10] By merging human consciousness with computers, we can dispense with bodies altogether and thereby avoid the body's inevitable decline. The second strategy, which seeks to alter humans at the cellular or genetic level, belongs in the realm of "life-extension science" and "bio-gerontology." In general, anti-aging research targets the genes that regulate aging and seeks ways to extend the life of cells in the human body.[11] The third strategy is to develop bionic devices that could replace limited or fragile body parts. Prostheses and organ transplantations are commonplace today, but many transhumanists believe there will come a day when we are able to replace body parts with machines or through cellular regeneration, before they fail or wear out.[12]

Although some of the ambitions of transhumanists sound fantastical, the leading figures of this movement work at prestigious universities and well-funded companies, which spend huge sums of money and resources developing transhumanist technologies. Billionaires such as Larry Ellison, CEO of Oracle Corpora-

---

[10] Ray Kurzweil, *The Singularity Is Near: When Humans Transcend Biology* (New York: Penguin Books, 2006).

[11] See Gregory M. Fahy et al., eds., *The Future of Aging: Pathways to Human Life Extension* (Dordrecht: Springer, 2010); and Karen Weintraub, "Researchers Study 3 Promising Anti-Aging Therapies," *Scientific American* (1 July 2015) http://www.scientificamerican.com/article/researchers-study-3-promising-anti-aging-therapies/.

[12] Mark Honigsbaum, "The Future of Robotics: In a Transhuman World, the Disabled Will Be the Ones Without Prosthetic Limbs," *The Guardian* (15 June 2013) http://www.theguardian.com/technology/2013/jun/16/future-robotics-bionic-limbs-disabled.

tion, Peter Thiel, co-founder of PayPal, and Sergey Brin, co-founder of Google, are financing research that promises to radically extend the human lifespan and eliminate death. "Death makes me very angry," Ellison says. "It doesn't make any sense to me. Death has never made any sense to me. How can a person be there and then just vanish, just not be there?"[13] Google, who employs Kurzweil as its Director of Engineering and has been a corporate backer of the Singularity University since 2008, has begun its own anti-aging biotech company, Calico, which reportedly aims to "solve death."[14]

Transhumanism has been criticized on a number of fronts, including the practical issues of access, justice, and voluntariness, as well as on its underlying philosophy. Some have criticized transhumanism for ignoring the potential social injustices that could result when the human race is divided between humans and post-humans, or "biological haves and have-nots."[15] In a world where some can pay to enhance their cognitive and physical attributes, access to these technologies may create a further divide between those who can or cannot afford such enhancements. The cost of becoming a post-human could lead to a loss of equal op-

---

[13] Adam Leith Gollner, "The Immortality Financiers: The Billionaires Who Want to Live Forever," *The Daily Beast* (20 Aug. 2013) http://www.thedailybeast.com/the-immortality-financiers-the-billionaires-who-want-to-live-forever.

[14] Harry McCracken and Lev Grossman, "Google vs. Death" online article http://content.time.com/subscriber/article/0,33009,2152422,00.html. *Time Magazine* (20 Sept. 2013); and Arion McNicoll, "How Google's Calico Aims to Fight Aging and 'Solve Death'," *CNN Tech* (3 Oct. 2013) http://www.cnn.com/2013/10/03/tech/innovation/google-calico-aging-death/.

[15] Keith Bauer, "Transhumanism and Its Critics: Five Arguments Against a Post-Human Future," *International Journal of Technoethics* 1/3 (2010): 1–10, 6.

portunity and the destabilization of democracy.[16]

Moreover, the voluntary nature of transhumanist technologies is suspect. Transhumanists such as Nick Bostrom are adamant that the use of enhancement technologies will be voluntary, which will help them to escape the legacy of eugenics. The idea that individuals make purely autonomous choices about their health and well-being that are wholly separate from the social and political forces that shape the healthcare landscape, however, underestimates the powers of biopolitics in our society. Far too often, technologies that were created to be freely chosen become legally, or at least socially, obligatory. For example, many women today report they feel immense pressure from their doctors to receive fetal ultrasounds or other tests that detect fetal anomalies, even when they say the results will not change their medical planning.[17] Some bioethicists have even suggested parents are morally required to undertake genetic interventions to prevent "harmful conditions to their offspring."[18] Although enhancements may seem less morally obligatory than tests and interventions that can diagnose and treat illness, in a world where enhancements are prevalent, it will be hard to compete with persons whose intelligence and physiology are greatly enhanced through biotechnology.[19] It is not hard to

---

[16] Ibid., 7.

[17] Kristin Zeiler, "Reproductive Autonomous Choice—a Cherished Illusion? Reproductive Autonomy Examined in the Context of Preimplantation Genetic Diagnosis," *Medicine Health Care and Philosophy* 7/2 (2004): 175–83; and Anita Ho, "The Individualist Model of Autonomy and the Challenge of Disability," *Journal of Bioethical Inquiry* 5/2–3 (2008): 193.

[18] Allen Buchanan et al., *From Chance to Choice: Genetics and Justice* (Cambridge: Cambridge University Press, 2000) 257.

[19] Although surely, many people do feel pressure to have cosmetic surgery (an enhancement) to meet ever-rising beauty standards, and young people feel pressure to use prescription (an enhancement) to enhance their cognitive performance.

image that if transhumanist technologies become prevalent, parents who refuse to enhance the lives of their children will be viewed as morally suspect.

On a more fundamental level, some critics claim the transhumanist conception of the human is problematic, because it reduces the complexity of the human being to biology or to the rational mind.[20] The idea that we could upload our consciousness into a computer reveals an understanding of the world wherein bodies and social environments are essentially irrelevant to identity construction, or that somehow an essential self is preserved without a body or a community in which one is intimately involved. Transhumanist discourse seems radically out of touch with phenomenological, feminist, black, disability, and other discourses, which stress the importance of the body as central to identity formation. Underlying much of the transhumanist discourse is an apparent ambivalence toward the human body.

Along these same lines, transhumanism also betrays an understanding of nature that reduces it to a mere resource of power. As is true of many post-Enlightenment thinkers, transhumanists see little value or meaning inherent in nature. Whereas nature was once thought to be imbued with its own meaning and purpose, nature, including human nature, is now seen as a power to be harnessed and controlled, an efficient cause to be used toward human ends.[21] Without any inherent purpose or meaning, the human body can be altered or refashioned in any way the transhumanist chooses. According to Brent Waters's description, "[Transhumanism] exemplifies and amplifies the technological and nihilistic ontology of late modernity in which the creation and its creatures are

---

[20] Bauer, "Transhumanism and Its Critics," 7.

[21] Jeffrey P. Bishop, "Transhumanism, Metaphysics, and the Post-Human God," *Journal of Medicine and Philosophy* 36/6 (2010): 700–20.

subjected to an endless and violent process of construction, deconstruction, and reconstruction."[22] For those who believe—for reasons theological or otherwise—nature has its own meaning or integrity apart from the human will to power, transhumanist metaphysics may be troubling.

CHRISTIAN TRANSHUMANISM

On the surface, it is rather unclear how Christian theology would find any commonality with the transhumanist agenda. As previously mentioned, most transhumanists identify as atheists. Moreover, they seem to advance two obviously heretical positions: the Manichean belief that the material body is an obstacle to full human flourishing, and the Pelagian belief that humans can perfect themselves.[23] Moreover, one would think that if Christians, particularly mainline liberal Protestants who tend to be most open to transhumanism, knew their own history, they would recognize their embrace of the American Eugenics movement shares a similar motivation to their embrace of transhumanism. Social Gospel proponents who supported eugenics in the early twentieth century also wanted to use the best of contemporary science to help improve the human condition and usher in the Kingdom of God.[24] The parallels are striking, but rarely explored.

Western Christianity and transhumanism, however, share a common philosophical legacy as well as some overlapping goals worth exploring. Transhumanism is a relatively new movement,

---

[22] Brent Waters, "Whose Salvation, Which Eschatology?" in *Transhumanism and Transcendence: Christian Hope in an Age of Technological Enhancement*, ed. Ronald Core-Turner (Washington D.C.: Georgetown University Press, 2011) 174.

[23] Waters, "Whose Salvation, Which Eschatology?" 170–71.

[24] Christine Rosen, *Preaching Eugenics: Religious Leaders and the American Eugenics Movement* (Oxford: Oxford University Press, 2004).

but it shares in many of our long-held cultural anxieties concerning death and our ambitions to cure disease, which is partly why some Christians have found it appealing. The Christian Transhumanist Association describes its mission as "participating with God in the redemption, reconciliation, and renewal of the world."[25] Christian transhumanists say they want to use technology to help "heal the sick, give sight to the blind, help the deaf to hear, the lame to walk, give voice to the mute, and guide persons toward holistic betterment in community."[26] From early Church writings, it is clear that healing has always been part of the Christian mission. Moreover, the belief that Christians should use science to relieve human beings from the limits of fragility and mortality has a long history. Sir Francis Bacon (1561–1626), for example, was a proponent of using the scientific method to manipulate nature for the purpose of human ends. For Bacon, divine grace alone (not human effort) granted salvation. Rather than moral perfection, Bacon believed human effort ought to be directed toward the service of one's neighbor, which required an instrumental approach to nature.[27] From the belief that God gave nature for the preservation and enhancement of human life came a requirement that all scientific endeavors prioritize technological improvement of the human condition. Bacon understood these "improvements" to include "the prolongation of life, the restitution of youth in some degree, the retardation of age, the curing of disease counted incurable, and the

---

[25] "About," *Christian Transhumanist Association*, http://www.christian transhumanism.org/about.

[26] Christopher Benek, "Why Christians Should Embrace Transhumanism," *The Christian Post* (31 May 2015) http://www.christianpost.com/news/why-christians-should-embrace-transhumanism-139790/.

[27] Gerald P. McKenny, *To Relieve the Human Condition: Bioethics, Technology, and the Body* (Albany: State University of New York Press, 1997) 17.

mitigation of pain."[28] Modern Christians and transhumanists alike are inheritors of Bacon's understanding of the priorities of science, even if they remain unaware of its theological roots.

Christian transhumanists also recognize the human longing for something better than what our current life has to offer. They tap into the dissatisfaction nearly every person feels with their human limitations and they recognize the tragedies inherent in life. There are perhaps vulnerabilities humans have that they would be better off without. Anyone who has ever suffered through a debilitating illness or seen a child die prematurely recognizes that eliminating certain effects of human vulnerability is not heretical, but an authentic Christian longing for a better world. Surely, technology can be and should be part of the betterment of society. Most Christians and transhumanists share the belief that evolution does not guarantee human flourishing and we should sometimes use technology to control evolution. Most Christian transhumanists do not seek to adopt the transhumanist agenda wholesale; rather, they believe they can use their God-given creativity to help direct transhumanism toward a better and more ethical course. Christians might help the transhumanist movement by figuring out how to use transhumanist technologies for Christ's redemptive purposes, rather than for self-gain. Alternatively, Christians might help transhumanists see the resonances between their project and the Christian Gospel, as Tillich did with other medico-scientific projects.[29]

In addition to the secular critiques already mentioned, Chris-

---

[28] Francis Bacon, "Magnalia Naturae," in *The Advancement of Learning and New Atlantis*, ed. Arthur Johnston (Oxford: Clarendon Press, 1974) 249.

[29] See Terry D. Cooper, *Paul Tillich and Psychology: Historic and Contemporary Explorations in Theology, Psychotherapy, and Ethics* (Macon GA: Mercer, 2006).

tian theologians have cautioned against fully adopting the trans-humanist agenda for at least three reasons: the created goodness of the body, the human tendency toward sin, and the transfor-mation/resurrection of the body promised by Jesus. A number of theologians have pointed out that both the Creation and Incarna-tion narratives point to the goodness of embodiment as well as human nature. Gerald McKenny argues, "In all its vulnerability, neediness, and finite limitation, and in spite of its corruption by sin, human nature is good, and is to be recognized and valued as such, because it is the being with this nature whom God has cho-sen to enjoy the highest form of communion with God."[30] In the Genesis narrative, God proclaims the world is good and, thus, human nature is not something to be overcome, even if God's cre-ations do not always represent that goodness. We do not need to become some other kind of being—a post-human—to receive God's grace or participate in the good life. Humans were "created and equipped" to commune with God, which is the telos of hu-man life.[31] Some have even argued finitude itself is good. In our finitude, we are reminded that we "are creatures who are created by a creator, and not self-made artifacts."[32] Moreover, by becom-ing Incarnate, Christ confirmed that neither the human body nor human nature is abhorrent. To despise our nature would be to despise what God has given and the very nature to which God has promised ultimate communion through Christ's redeeming action.

The human capacity for sin also places a necessary caution on the telos of the transhumanist project. Many transhumanists, such

---

[30] Gerald McKenny, "Transcendence, Technological Enhancement, and Christian Theology," in *Transhumanism and Transcendence: Christian Hope in an Age of Technological Enhancement*, ed. Ronald Core-Turner (Washington D.C.: Georgetown University Press, 2011) 187.

[31] Ibid., 185.

[32] Waters, "Whose Salvation, Which Eschatology?" 174.

as Ray Kurzweil, imagine that post-human existence will solve the world's major problems such as "war, hunger, poverty, death, and disease."[33] Some transhumanists agree their project requires ethical oversight to ensure it does not become corrupted,[34] but few acknowledge "humanity's unexplained but inescapable tendency to pervert and destroy even its best achievements..."[35] As sinful creatures, we tend to distort the good into our selfish desires. Without the wisdom to know what God desires for our lives, we are even liable to misunderstand what is good for us. Moreover, the idea that we will be able to fashion ourselves to our own desires overlooks the radical ways in which God promises to transform us. The Christian vision of the "good life" is not one wherein all our greatest desires for ourselves are fulfilled, but one in which we participate in God's transformation of our desires. In preparation for God's Kingdom, Christians practice self-emptying, not self-fulfillment.[36] While none of these critiques necessitates that Christians must reject all transhumanist projects, they do add a necessary note of caution to those Christians who find an easy correlation between transhumanism and the Christian life.

TILLICH, SCIENCE, AND ULTIMATE CONCERN

Tillich's critiques of certain scientific pursuits in his own time echo the critiques of transhumanism mentioned above. Tillich not only lived through World War II, he was dismissed from his

---

[33] Ray Kurzweil, *The Age of Spiritual Machines: When Computers Exceed Human Intelligence* (London: Penguin Books, 2000) 280.

[34] Bostrom, "Transhumanist Values," 12.

[35] Ronald Cole-Turner, ed., "Transhumanism and Christianity," in *Transhumanism and Transcendence: Christian Hope in an Age of Technological Enhancement*, (Washington D.C.: Georgetown University Press, 2011) 194–95.

[36] Ibid., 199.

teaching position at the University of Frankfurt for speaking out against the Nazi movement.[37] Given what happened in Germany, Tillich was wary of utopian projects that promised to bring to power a new class of superhumans. Although the post-human is not simply the Übermensch in disguise (although some transhumanists do believe the post-human will be an instantiation of Nietzsche's Übermensch[38]), given his history, there is reason to believe Tillich would have been wary of the utopian leanings of transhumanism.

At the same time, Tillich's method of correlation, which seeks out the latent spiritual depth present in contemporary cultural formations, may be attractive to Christians who identify elements of the transhumanist movement with elements of the Christian message. As an apologetic theologian, Tillich believed theology must use the eternal message of the Christian Gospel to answer existential questions posed by humans in various cultural forms.[39] Transhumanism, insofar as it presumes to know what makes us human, what elements of human nature are undesirable, and what our goals for living should be, is exactly the kind of cultural formation to which Tillich believed theology should respond. Clearly, most Christian transhumanists do not simply take up the transhumanist agenda uncritically; rather, they identify with the parts of the movement that appear to resonate with their own understanding of the Christian mission to heal and reveal the Kingdom of God on earth. In a similar fashion, Tillich used his method of correlation to analyze depth psychology, which he believed

---

[37] Wilhelm Pauck and Marion Pauck, *Paul Tillich: His Life & Thought* (Eugene: Wipf and Stock, 1976).

[38] Max More, "Technological Self-Transformation: Expanding Personal Extropy," *Extropy* 4/2 (1993): http://www.maxmore.com/selftrns.htm.

[39] Paul Tillich, *Systematic Theology*, 3 vols. (Chicago: University of Chicago Press, 1951–1963) 1:3.

contained truths that were compatible with the truths of the Christian message. As I will show, however, Tillich's writings on religion as ultimate concern add to, rather than reduce, the moral ambivalence Christians may feel about the transhumanist agenda.

We should perhaps not be surprised whenever a movement that appreciates both religion and science should cite Tillich as one of its vanguards. Tillich did not believe science and religion were necessarily in conflict, because they dealt with different dimensions of meaning within reality.[40] Christian transhumanists recognize there is no necessary conflict between scientific research that seeks to understand the mechanisms behind aging and illness and the Christian message. To be credible to a culture that appreciates science, Christians must not appear as though they are opposed to science or stand in the way of scientific discovery for theological reasons.[41] Today, perhaps more than ever, our cultural situation is shaped by the techno- and medico-sciences. If theologians wish to speak to the culture in which they live, they must understand how the culture is shaped by the sciences. Tillich's method of correlation is supremely suited to this endeavor, because it clearly expresses how theology should relate to the sciences. For example, when discussing mental illness, Tillich writes, "Theology is not concerned with the spread of mental diseases or with our increasing awareness of them, but it *is* concerned with the psychiatric interpretation of these trends."[42] Today, Tillich might say that theology is not concerned with the science behind aging research, but it is concerned with the transhumanist interpretation of

---

[40] Paul Tillich, *Dynamics of Faith*, Perennial Classics (New York: Harper Collins, 2001 [1957]) 94.

[41] John F. Haught, "Tillich in Dialogue with Natural Science," in *The Cambridge Companion to Paul Tillich*, ed. Russell Re Manning (Cambridge: Cambridge University Press, 2009) 223–37.

[42] Tillich, *Systematic Theology*, 1:4.

aging and mortality as limitations to be corrected.

Tillich's method of correlation does not allow theologians to accept scientific pursuits uncritically, even the ones that appear to confirm the truths of faith. Religion and science are two fields that employ different methods to arrive at truth. The failure to understand that religion and science deal with different dimensions of reality has caused some to believe that religion and science are opposing explanations of truth. When religion and science have come into conflict, it is typically because of an epistemological confusion. On the one hand, Christians have sometimes mistaken the symbols of the faith for literal descriptions, such as when they have read the book of Genesis as a historical account of the beginning of the world.[43] Scientists can also err, however, when they attempt to use the scientific method to explain matters of faith. God, for example, cannot be understood by the scientific method, because God is not an object within the world or a cause alongside other causes—instead, according to Tillich, God is the ground of being or being itself.[44] Science understands reality in terms of objectifiable materiality. To know the world scientifically, we must objectify it; to know God, we must be grasped by something we cannot contain. Any attempt to know God or understand faith through the modes of scientific understanding immediately becomes idolatrous.

Although separate disciplines, theology and science both require an ontological foundation. In determining what is a disease or what behaviors are pathological, scientists, whether they realize it or not, rely on an understanding of human nature. Theologians should be attuned to how the medical sciences fail to be explicit about their underlying ontologies. Tillich explains,

---

[43] Tillich, *Dynamics of Faith*, 94–95.
[44] Tillich, *Systematic Theology*, 2:6–7.

[Medicine] includes a decision about the nature of man which must be made explicit, in spite of the positivistic resistance to ontology...[the psychiatrist] cannot avoid the question of human nature since in practicing his profession he cannot avoid the distinction between health and illness, existential and pathological anxiety.... The medical faculty needs a doctrine of man in order to fulfill its theoretical task; and it cannot have a doctrine of man without the permanent cooperation of all those faculties whose central object is man.[45]

Today, neither theologians nor medical scientists are likely to admit they require an ontology, but insofar as each attempts to interpret human existence, theology and medicine must join philosophy.[46] In his own time, Tillich saw the lack of ontological analysis as preventing ministers and physicians from cooperating. Today, the lack of ontological analysis amongst both scientists and theologians likely prevents them from engaging one another with the rigor and seriousness each deserves.

Along with ontologies, scientific pursuits can express elements of faith. Scientific movements can become faith movements when adherents fail to appreciate the scope of the scientific discipline and attempt to explain the whole of reality using the scientific method. In other words, science can express an ultimate concern—something for which a person is willing to sacrifice everything.[47] Tillich writes, for example, "If representatives of modern physics reduce the whole of reality to the mechanical movement of the smallest particles of matter, denying the really

---

[45] Paul Tillich, *The Courage to Be*, 3rd ed. (New Haven: Yale University Press, 2014 [1952]) 71.

[46] Ibid., 72.

[47] Tillich, *Dynamics of Faith*, 94.

real quality of life and mind, they express a faith, objectively as well as subjectively."[48] The symbol of this faith is a universe that is reduced to "a meaningless mechanism."[49] As critics have pointed out, much of transhumanism is reductionistic, both in terms of how it understands nature (including human nature) and in terms of human identity. By reducing life to mere biology or the conscious, rational mind, transhumanists risk missing the spiritual and social dimensions of life altogether. Tillich's understanding of ultimate concern may lead Christians to see transhumanism as expressing faith commitments.

Along with elements of ontology and faith, transhumanists reveal a teleology when they endorse enhancements that will improve the human condition and create a desirable post-human existence. The transhumanist teleology also contains elements of faith and not mere scientific assertions. To presume that there is an objective good in prolonging life or enhancing certain human characteristics requires an idea of what constitutes the "good life," which is the domain of philosophers and theologians. Determining which characteristics should be "enhanced" and the social implications of dramatically increasing the average lifespan requires that theologian-philosophers and scientists work together in determining which technologies should be pursued—particularly when massive amounts of money, both private and public, are being invested in these technologies.

We must be careful in allowing the medical sciences to determine what is perfect or even good for the human being. Tillich warns that science also stands under the ambiguity of life—it simply does not have all the answers. In examining the transhumanist telos, Christians should have special concern for those per-

---

[48] Ibid.
[49] Ibid., 95.

sons who will be disadvantaged by the quest to perfect human-kind. For example, to the transhumanist, disability can only be seen as tragic, because it already has an idea of the perfect dis-embodied or the technologically enhanced body. Persons who strive for human immortality and perfection can rarely tolerate the imperfect, even though they claim enhancement technologies will be optional for individuals.[50] Tillich, on the other hand, thought perfection was ambiguous. Our desire for bodily, mental, or physi-cal perfection fosters new utopias, which have as much potential to enslave as to liberate.[51] In their quest to enhance and perfect, the transhumanist is unlikely to see the beauty or perfection that may come when a disabled child is accepted, befriended, and brought into the eucharistic community.

According to Tillich, theologians and philosophers are uniquely able to distinguish elements of faith within a scientific project or movement and should do so when the lines between science and faith become blurred or when scientists use their own elements of faith to attack other forms of faith.[52] Theologians, therefore, should be wary when transhumanists claim their move-ment is not a practice of faith or a religion and that it can rest easi-ly alongside other faith traditions. Zoltan Istvan, political candi-date for the Transhumanist party (and more recently for the Libertarian party),[53] for example, claims transhumanism is not a

---

[50] Waters, "Whose Salvation? Which Eschatology?" 171.

[51] Eduardo R. Cruz, "The Quest for Perfection: Insight from Paul Til-lich," in *Is Nature Ever Evil? Religion, Science, and Value*, ed. Willem B. Drees (London: Routledge, 2003) 214–24.

[52] Tillich, *Dynamics of Faith*, 97.

[53] More libertarian transhumanists such as Nick Bostrom believe trans-humanism can escape the legacy of eugenics by keeping the government out of the project, and making it all about personal choice, but with its own po-litical party and a presidential candidate, it is clear some transhumanists de-sire more government influence. See Zoltan Istvan, "Transhumanists and

religion or in competition with religion. Although an outspoken atheist who has criticized nearly all world religions for promoting a "Deathist culture,"[54] Istvan recognizes most Americans—along with most of the world—adhere to a religious faith, and he has recently (in conjunction with his political campaigns) become more open to Christians who embrace transhumanism. Istvan has written he believes the Bible "supports humans improving themselves," which is also the goal of transhumanism.[55] Christians, however, ought to be skeptical of such superficial claims. Simply because some of the claims of Christians and transhumanists overlap does not mean their ultimate telos or underlying ontologies are identical.

KURZWEIL AND FAITH IN THE SINGULARITY

One of the most influential figures of the transhumanist movement is Ray Kurzweil, a self-proclaimed inventor and futurist. Kurzweil does not call himself a transhumanist or posthumanist, mainly because he believes the future he imagines will still be composed of "humans," albeit in a drastically altered form.[56] Still, what Kurzweil imagines as the future state of humankind aligns with the World Transhumanist Association's vision. Kurzweil's influential work, *The Singularity Is Near*, outlines

---

Libertarians Have Much in Common," *Huffington Post* (5 May 2014) http://www.huffingtonpost.com/zoltan-istvan/transhumanism-and-libertarianism_b_5248966.html.

[54] Zoltan Istvan, "Can Transhumanism Overcome a Widespread Deathist Culture?" *Huffington Post* (26 May 2015) http://www.huffingtonpost.com/zoltan-istvan/can-transhumanism-overcom_b_7433108.html.

[55] Zoltan Istvan, "An Atheist's Perspective on the Rise of Christian Transhumanism," *Huffington Post* (6 Mar. 2015) http://www.huffingtonpost.com/zoltan-istvan/an-atheists-perspective-o_b_6802140.html.

[56] Kurzweil, *The Singularity Is Near*, 374.

his views on the evolution of humankind, technology, and the ultimate destiny of the universe. The "Singularity" for Kurzweil refers to the era in which humans will "transcend [the] limitations of our biological bodies and brains" by merging ourselves with non-biological intelligence to become infinitely more intelligent and creative.[57] Examining Kurzweil's work through Tillich's understanding of ultimate concern reveals how many faith elements are present in his technological project.

Kurzweil claims being a "Singularitarian"—or accepting what he believes about the future in the Singularity—is not a matter of faith; rather, it is an understanding of the world based on his analysis of scientific trends.[58] Kurzweil admits to only one belief as foundational to his project: the belief that the universe exists. "I believe that the universe exists," he writes. "That's my personal leap of faith.... I don't know that anything exists other than my own thoughts."[59] Kurzweil's metaphysical presumption that the universe is really real might be considered a matter of belief rather than fact, but this is not the only belief statement Kurzweil expresses. In fact, Kurzweil has many latent belief statements concerning the nature of the world and humankind, which are not based on empirical or scientific understandings alone. Kurzweil claims to understand the nature of humans, the nature of the universe, the ultimate destiny of both humans and the universe, and what makes life meaningful. His faith statements present as an ultimate concern as Tillich understands it.

Kurzweil begins *The Singularity Is Near* with an overview of what he believes are the six great epochs in the history of the evolution. Much like Christian dispensationalism, which divides bib-

---

[57] Ibid., 9.
[58] Ibid., 370.
[59] Ibid., 389–90.

lical history into distinct periods of significance for Christians (including future periods), Kurzweil divides up the history of the universe into distinct epochs that move toward the final destiny of the universe. Epoch one traces our origins in physics and chemistry, where information is represented in its basic structures. Epoch two is "biology," where this information gets encoded in DNA. In Epoch three, the human brain forms as the evolution of information into consciousness. In Epoch four, intelligent humans begin to use technology.[60] In Epoch five, human technology will merge with human intelligence (the beginning of the Singularity).[61] Finally, in Epoch six, the universe will "wake up" or be infused with intelligence, which Kurzweil claims is "...the ultimate destiny of the Singularity and the universe."[62] Kurzweil can be confident in his reading of history in part because of two unstated beliefs integral to his project: the essential element of life is information and the telos of all matter is intelligence. The belief that life can be reduced to information patterns, and the telos of matter is intelligence are not empirically verifiable facts; rather, they are metaphysical beliefs.

As is clear in his epochal interpretation of history, Kurzweil believes "patterns of information" are what define life. Physics and chemistry represent basic information, biology is information in DNA, brains are information in neural patters, and technology is information in hardware and software designs. Meaningful life can be boiled down to *information*. As many popular scientific writers are inclined to do, Kurzweil speaks of evolution (before human intervention) as an agent moving life toward patterned order. He

---

[60] Ibid., 15–16.
[61] Ibid., 20.
[62] Ibid., 21.

speaks of evolution as "increasing order,"[63] creating innovation,[64] developing protection mechanisms,[65] and "recording and manipulating information."[66] Unlike many other scientific readings of evolutionary history, which reduce organisms to products of history indistinguishable from artifacts,[67] Kurzweil retains an understanding of final causes. Although conscious humans eventually take over the job of evolution, Kurzweil's epochal reading of evolution endows it with a teleological purpose to which the universe has been moving. This is no mere objective reading of history; evolution (as an agent) moves the universe toward intelligence.

Thus, while information is the essential element of life, intelligence is the telos of all matter. It is no wonder that Kurzweil believes we can remain essentially human without our bodies—the brain is the most important system in our bodies.[68] Minds uploaded into computers are still human, because intelligence defines what it means to be human. Kurzweil believes we will one day infuse the entire universe, even "dumb" matter, with our intelligence: "As I see it, the *purpose* of the universe reflects the same *purpose* as our lives: to move toward greater intelligence and knowledge… Once we saturate the matter and energy in the universe with intelligence, it will 'wake up,' be conscious, and sublimely intelligent. That's about as close to God as I can imagine."[69] For Kurzweil, evolution might lack a formal cause, but it certainly has an efficient, material, and final cause. This addition of a final cause is

---

[63] Ibid., 40.

[64] Ibid.

[65] Ibid., 42.

[66] Ibid., 40.

[67] Michael Hanby, *No God, No Science? Theology, Cosmology, Biology* (Oxford: Wiley-Blackwell, 2013) 206.

[68] Kurzweil, *The Singularity Is Near*, 307–308.

[69] Ibid., 372 (emphasis mine).

metaphysically notable, because it is not commonly held in contemporary science. For many, final causes are the realm of theology, because final causes explain the purpose of life. Kurzweil, however, is all too eager to define what makes life purposeful or meaningful. According to Kurzweil, "The explosion of art, science, and other forms of knowledge that the Singularity will bring will make life more than bearable; it will make life truly meaningful."[70] Not only does Kurzweil have an understanding of the telos of all matter, he also presumes to know what makes life meaningful, which wanders into the realm of ethics. Such statements go beyond mere scientific assertions; these are metaphysical and ethical concepts that demand theological engagement.

For Kurzweil, the Singularity is his ultimate concern. Not only does he devote his career to pursuing technologies that will help usher in the Singularity and proselytizing its inevitability to others, he has changed his entire lifestyle to ensure he is alive to see the Singularity occur. He takes 250 supplements a day and half a dozen intravenous therapies a week to ensure he will live long enough to witness the "biotechnology revolution."[71] Kurzweil believes his "sacrifice" will be rewarded with participation in the Singularity. Kurzweil might not believe in God, but the elements of his faith certainly function as a religion.

UTOPIANISM, THE KINGDOM OF GOD, AND
THE AMBIGUITY OF TECHNOLOGY

Kurzweil is hardly singular in his devotion to the technological future, and he may not be wrong about where we are headed as a species.[72] Whether or not this is the direction we *should* head,

---

[70] Ibid.

[71] Ibid., 211–12.

[72] Various authors debate how accurate Kurzweil's predictions about the

however, is debatable. Theologians who wish to engage transhumanism ought to be aware of the belief statements embedded in
the project so they can find points of common interest as well as
points of departure. One element of faith in particular that ought
to be analyzed by theologians is the latent utopianism expressed by
many transhumanists. The transhumanist vision of the post-
human (whether that be the biologically and morally enhanced
human or the human whose mind lives inside a super-machine)
does not align easily with the Christian notion of the Kingdom of
God. It is incumbent upon Christians to discern whether the
transhumanist telos verges on idolatry, or taking a preliminary
concern as ultimate.[73] Tillich writes,

> In true faith the ultimate concern is a concern about the truly
> ultimate; while in idolatrous faith preliminary, finite realities
> are elevated to the rank of ultimacy. The inescapable conse-
> quence of idolatrous faith is 'existential disappointment,' a
> disappointment which penetrates into the very existence of
> man![74]

Although Tillich did not necessarily believe in an afterlife or
believe that the Kingdom of God was a culminating singular event
that will happen at the end of time, he did find the Kingdom of
God to be a powerful symbol of the convergence of the eternal and
temporal. In Tillich's theology, the Kingdom of God has never
been identical to life-extension or even everlasting life. Instead,
eschatological questions contain within them presumptions about
"the *telos* of everything that is."[75] The promise of technology, such
as the technologies of transhumanism, can create a utopian fantasy

---

future have been.
[73] Tillich, *Systematic Theology*, 1:13.
[74] Tillich, *Dynamics of Faith*, 13.
[75] Tillich, *Systematic Theology*, 3:298.

that lures us into believing our salvation is just around the corner.[76] Tillich did not believe we found total fulfillment in this life; rather, we only get fragmentary moments. It is unlikely that Tillich would have seriously accepted the post-human—a person who never ages or dies—would be the final fulfillment of humankind. Instead, for every victory we must be ready for a new demonic power to arise.[77] Our freedom allows us to contradict our essential nature as well as our own fulfillment.[78]

For Tillich, an examination of the twentieth century reveals the problematic character of idolatrous utopian interpretations of history.[79] The atrocities committed by the Nazis along with the failure of the Social Gospel movement (whose adherents largely supported the American Eugenics Movement[80]) weakened the symbol of the Kingdom of God.[81] Twenty-first-century transhumanists, however, rarely see the connections between their own project and the failed utopianism of the twentieth century. Analogously, detached or largely unaware of Christian leaders' involvement in the American eugenics movement, few Christian transhumanists make a connection between the utopian fantasies of the early twentieth century and their own. Far from supporting a utopian vision, Tillich did not believe there would ever be a time in which all ambiguities in life are conquered. Belief in a perfect future or a perfect body will inevitably lead to disappointment:

---

[76] Paul Tillich, "The Decline and the Validity of Progress," in *The Spiritual Situation in our Technical Society*, ed. J. Mark Thomas (Macon GA: Mercer, 1988) 93.

[77] Ibid., 94.

[78] Ibid., 95.

[79] Tillich, *Systematic Theology*, 3:354.

[80] See Rosen, *Preaching Eugenics: Religious Leaders and the American Eugenics Movement*, 16.

[81] Tillich, *Systematic Theology*, 3:357.

Existential disappointments produce individual and social diseases and catastrophes: the price for idolatrous ecstasy must be paid. For utopianism, taken literally, is idolatrous. It gives the quality of ultimacy to something preliminary. It makes unconditional what is conditioned (a future historical situation) and at the same time disregards the always-present existential estrangement and the ambiguities of life and history. This makes the utopian interpretation of history inadequate and dangerous.[82]

Against the idea that transhumanist technologies will be autonomously chosen and, therefore, escape the legacy of eugenics, Tillich reminds us, "We must not forget that democracy can produce a mass conformity which is more dangerous for the dynamic element in history and its revolutionary expression than is an openly working absolutism. The Kingdom of God is as hostile to established conformism as it is to negativistic non-conformism."[83] As previously mentioned, transhumanists' belief that informed consent and autonomy are ethically sufficient to ensure that technologies will be *optional* choices is naïve. Bioethicists, who promote the principle of autonomy, sometimes forget that simply because people provide consent, does not make their choices ethical.

Christians should be wary of assuming transhumanist technologies will be good for individuals or society as a whole, but they should also be open to the possibility that such technologies express a latent spiritual depth—or share in our culture's deep desire for connection and health. Tillich believed technology was a miracle of the modern age when it was used to relieve "unrelenting stress of bodily pain, from stifling oppression of the daily evils of the natural process, and from the defenselessness with which the

---

[82] Ibid., 3:355.
[83] Ibid., 3:389.

earliest human beings were abandoned to nature."[84] Moreover, Tillich acknowledged technology has transformed our world and that we must learn to incorporate it into the "ultimate meaning of life."[85] He believed technology has the power to "de-demonize" things that once provoked fear and oppression.[86] Technology itself can be godlike, in that it can be creative and liberating. Our technical productions represent a new creation and a new form of being that we bring into the world.[87] Tillich also believed technology's ability to create human community across space and time provided modern people with eschatological hope.[88] As someone who was not so sure about "life after death," Tillich may have appreciated the transhumanist ambition to bring futuristic hope to the here and now.

Of course, technology can also destroy. As Tillich preached, "The greatest triumph of science was the power it gave to man to annihilate himself and his world."[89] Theology must give voice to both the constructive and destructive potentialities inherent in scientific progress, particularly in the power of biotechnologies to heal individuals and end unnecessary suffering, but also annihilate humankind and make us strangers to ourselves. Humans create to make their place in a strange world. We build to stave off the uncanniness of life, but our homes and cities retain their sense of the

---

[84] Paul Tillich, "The Freedom of Science," in *The Spiritual Situation in our Technical Society*, ed. J. Mark Thomas (Macon GA: Mercer, 1988) 60.

[85] Ibid.

[86] Ibid.

[87] Paul Tillich, "The Technical City as Symbol," in *The Spiritual Situation in our Technical Society*, ed. J. Mark Thomas (Macon GA: Mercer, 1988) 182.

[88] Tillich, "The Freedom of Science," 60.

[89] Paul Tillich, "The Shaking of the Foundations," in *The Shaking of the Foundations*, ed. Paul Tillich (New York: Charles Scribner's Sons, 1955).

uncanny.[90] How much more is this true when our project is our own body? To feel more at home in our bodies, we invent technologies to spare us from the fragility and strangeness of life, and in so doing, we risk making our bodies into something foreign to us. It is unlikely we will ever feel at home in the mind of a computer or even a body that refuses to age. Our own best efforts to create bodies to fit our will and fulfill our desires may very well produce bodies that are strangers to us.[91]

If he were alive, would Tillich call himself a transhumanist? I doubt it, but he may have found room for a correlational response to the deep questions transhumanism raises about finitude and embodiment. Transhumanism has an ultimate concern, along with an ontology and teleology, but it does not perfectly align with Tillich's own. For those theologians, bioethicists, and scientists who wish to carry on Tillich's method of correlation, transhumanism represents a cultural manifestation that is revealing of the times we live in. More work must be done to unearth all of the ambitions, anxieties, and ambiguities that are revealed in the transhumanist project. Perhaps more urgently, however, to dismiss transhumanists outright would overlook the support—financial and otherwise—the movement has recently received from certain sectors of American society. What Tillich understood in his own time was that Christians cannot ignore other disciplines, much less popular cultural formations. Today, perhaps more than ever, our cultural situation is shaped by the techno- and medico-sciences, and Christianity ignores this reality at its peril.

---

[90] Tillich, "The Technical City as Symbol," 182.

[91] Transhumanist Julian Savalescu believes we could solve this problem through neurological moral enhancements, but my guess is Tillich would have his doubts. Julian Savalescu and Ingmar Persson, "Moral Enhancement, Freedom, and the God Machine," *Monist* 95/3 (2012): 399–421.

Index